MW01074189

Haunted
Washington

0 11557 00683 4

Haunted Washington

Ghosts and Strange Phenomena of the Evergreen State

Charles A. Stansfield Jr.

STACKPOLE
BOOKS

To Diane,
with all my love, always.

Copyright ©2011 by Stackpole Books

Published by
STACKPOLE BOOKS
5067 Ritter Road
Mechanicsburg, PA 17055
www.stackpolebooks.com

All rights reserved, including the right to reproduce this book or portions thereof in any form or by any means, electronic or mechanical, including photocopying, recording, or by any information storage and retrieval system, without permission in writing from the publisher. All inquiries should be addressed to Stackpole Books.

Printed in the United States of America

10 9 8 7 6 5 4 3 2 1

FIRST EDITION

Cover design by Tessa J. Sweigert

Illustrations by Marc Radle

Library of Congress Cataloging-in-Publication Data

Stansfield, Charles A.
  Haunted Washington : ghosts and strange phenomena of the evergreen state / Charles A. Stansfield Jr. — 1st ed.
      p. cm.
  Includes bibliographical references.
  ISBN-13: 978-0-8117-0683-4 (pbk.)
  ISBN-10: 0-8117-0683-4 (pbk.)
  1. Haunted places—Washington (State) 2. Ghosts—Washington (State) I. Title.
  BF1472.U6.S7285 2011
  133.109797—dc22
                                    2010038618

Contents

Contents

Introduction

GHOSTS, WITCHES, MONSTERS. WHY ARE WE SO FASCINATED BY THEM, even if we're not all sure that they really exist?

It is an interesting fact that every human group that now exists on the planet, or has ever existed, has traditions of supernatural people, creatures, and events. Tales of ghosts, witches, and monsters of all varieties are featured in the folklore of every society. No racial, ethnic, religious, or linguistic group of people anywhere lacks some history of interest in and concerns about the supernatural. Interest in the supernatural is thus universal; it cuts across both space and time. Often, even the specifics of pop cultural beliefs and stories can be startlingly similar. Dragons, for example, are common in both European and Chinese legends. They are even pictured in much the same way—as huge crocodilian-type reptiles, covered in scales, with clawed feet and long, toothy snouts. They even breathe fire. Is this pure coincidence?

Another theme, common to people living thousands of miles apart and separated by whole oceans and continents, is that of shape-shifting vampires. As portrayed in Eastern European traditions, vampires can shift from human form to bats or wolves. Six thousand miles away, the Navajo of Arizona tell of vampires or witches that can shape shift from humans to owls or wolves.

Many Native Americans, including those in the Pacific Northwest, have handed down stories about witches and witchcraft. Can some people acquire supernatural powers directly from the Devil himself? Four and five centuries ago, many Europeans were so convinced that witches lived among them that they hanged or burned at the stake alleged witches. In England alone, thirty thousand people were killed because their neighbors thought that they were witches. Housecats were thought to be "familiars" of witches, feline henchmen of evil, and creatures of Satan. In Europe, hundreds of thousands of cats were killed under that belief. Ironically, this slaughter of cats led to a rapid increase in rat populations—rats that spread the dreaded Black Death or bubonic plague. On the other side of the world, Japanese folklore tells of ghostly vampire cats—a truly fearsome image.

If legends of ghosts, witches, and monsters are universal among contemporary and historical cultures around the world, such beliefs are not necessarily held by every individual in any culture. People fit into one of three broad categories: true believers, confirmed skeptics, and those who are not certain. That third group may be the largest of all. There is an old story that a wise old man was asked if he believed in ghosts. "No," he replied, "but I am afraid of them." He was skeptical, but not looking forward to a face-to-face confrontation either.

Public fascination with the supernatural can be documented easily by scanning television program listings, ads for new films, and bestseller book lists. Phantoms, witches, demons, vampires, and monsters fascinate us. Even if we are profoundly skeptical, we can still enjoy a good story and shiver at a good scare. It has always been this way. In the venerable classic *Beowulf*, the hero must cope with a monster of seemingly supernatural power. William Shakespeare's *Macbeth* involves witchcraft, and *Hamlet* features a ghost. Halloween has been observed for more than a thousand years. As a modern holiday, it ranks second only to Christmas in consumer spending. Why do so many kids and adults dress up as ghosts, witches, vampires, and monsters? Perhaps we like to gently mock the mysteries of life, and of death, and so diminish our deepest fears and concerns about those topics. We reduce their mystery by joking about the nature of life and death.

Belief in ghosts, or at least a willingness to admit such beliefs, may be increasing. As related in Rosemary Ellen Guiley's *Encyclopedia of Ghosts and Spirits*, an 1889 survey conducted in England, France, Germany, and the United States reported that ten percent of the people polled had some contact with a ghost. A 1987 University of Chicago study showed forty-two percent of American adults—

and sixty-seven percent of widows—reported some form of contact with the dead.

A 1996 Gallup poll found that seventy-two of every one hundred Americans believe that there is intelligent life on other planets in the universe, and twenty-two percent think we're being visited by extraterrestrials. Seventy-one percent think that our government knows more about this than it will admit.

Where do you stand on the subjects of ghosts, witches, UFOs, and monsters? Are you a true believer, a confirmed skeptic, or one of those who are just not sure? You would fit best in the first or third groups if you have a lucky item of clothing or jewelry or believe in lucky numbers. If you believe in chance, luck, or magic, then you are recognizing that unseen, perhaps uncontrollable, forces have some degree of power over you and your fate. The word *superstition* comes from the Latin word *superstitio*, meaning soothsaying. *Soothsaying* refers to foretelling the future. An interest in foretelling the future implies that we don't control it, but that mysterious, supernatural forces shape our future.

The Evergreen State has a rich and varied paranormal past. In this book, the state has been divided into five regions for grouping the stories: Puget Sound Metropolitan Region, Olympic Peninsula and San Juan Islands, the Cascades, Northeast Washington, and Southeast Washington.

The Legend of Bigfoot

This creature, also known as Sasquatch and presumably a fellow primate, is said to roam the dense forests of Washington. It might as well be the official monster of the Evergreen State. In fact, in the western part of the state, everyone can agree on one thing: this is Bigfoot Country. Judging by the number of reported sightings, Bigfoot's favored habitat, again based on many alleged encounters going back centuries, includes the forests of the Pacific Northwest from northern California to British Columbia, and perhaps as far north as Alaska. To be fair, Bigfoot-type creatures have been spotted as far away as Florida, but the most famous and widely accepted sightings have been in three states: California, Oregon, and Washington.

Is Bigfoot real, in the sense that anyone can see for themselves hard, irrefutable evidence, such as a living specimen or an intact skeleton? No such conclusive evidence exists, at least not yet. On the other hand, eyewitness accounts are plentiful. Are these eyewitnesses all lying or deceived? There are numerous casts or photos of alleged Bigfoot footprints.

Then there is the famous, often-cited, and controversial Patterson-Gimblin film—less than a minute long—shot in northern California on October 20, 1967. The grainy 16-millimeter film is of poor quality. It shows the creature walking away from the camera, which is about eighty feet away, and glancing over to the side; its body is thick, and it has massive shoulders. The film has been examined intensively by scientists and anthropologists. More than forty years later, the consensus remains split. Some experts believe the subject is a man in a costume. Many Hollywood makeup artists, costumers, and special effects professionals say it was not a costume. In the film, the muscles can be seen flexing under the hairy pelt. Some professionals say that a man's muscles would be evident under a tight-fitting suit, although others contend that the artistically advanced costumes available in 1967 could not have duplicated this muscular movement. The creature's gait and length of stride have been judged by some as not human.

Another important question to ask is *could* Bigfoot be real? The lack of Bigfoot or Bigfoot-like ancestral fossils sometimes is cited by disbelievers as a major weakness in the case for Bigfoot. Why haven't we found fossilized bones of Bigfoot? This particular criticism, however, proves nothing. The overwhelming majority of Bigfoot descriptions are unequivocal on one point: Bigfoot is apelike—a primate. The fossil record is notoriously lacking any clear record of ancestry for modern chimpanzees, gorillas, or orangutans. These primates certainly exist, but we know almost nothing about their ancestry from fossils.

The fossil record, as spotty as it is, does at least prove that ancient primates ranged from primitive creatures the size of squirrels to giants larger than any known living gorillas or their relatives. Southern Asia once was home to *Gigantopithecus* ("Giant Ape"). These giants are known only through a few jaw fragments and a handful of teeth, but that is enough to say that they were closely related to modern orangutans and probably walked on two feet.

Most likely, *Gigantopithecus*, like chimpanzees, ate a variety of foods, including meat. At an estimated seven to eight feet tall, *Gigantopithecus* begins to sound a lot like most descriptions of Bigfoot. Could Bigfoot be a descendent of *Gigantopithecus* that crossed the Bering "land bridge" that once connected Asia and North America? There is, of course, no way to prove that possibility. What Giganto's fossils do prove without doubt is that primates can be that large.

There is another key question in regard to whether Bigfoot could exist: Is the habitat of North America, and specifically the Pacific Northwest, capable of supporting a creature like Bigfoot? The short answer must be yes.

Bigfoot's very size, estimated at between seven and ten feet tall, would seem to require large amounts of food. Would Bigfoot find enough to eat? Sure, assuming that Bigfoot, like his presumed primate cousins, eats both plants and animals. Moose, elk, bears, and mountain lions all thrive in Washington, most especially in the dense forests of the Olympic and Cascade ranges. Bigfoot's very large size, in fact, could well be an asset in its survival. Biologists cite Bergmann's Rule, which says that animals tend to have more body mass the further one moves from the equator and closer to arctic regions. More body mass keeps you warmer. Alaskan Kodiak bears and polar bears are much bigger and heavier than their cousins to the south. Siberian tigers outweigh Indian tigers. It is the smallest mammals, shrews, that must eat the highest proportion of food to body weight every day. Larger animals don't need as much food in proportion to their size. Then, too, larger animals can eat large quantities of nutrient-poor, low-calorie bulk foods that smaller animals cannot process.

Assuming that Bigfoot is neither supernatural nor immortal, there can't just be one—there must be a breeding population in the hundreds, if not thousands. If the fossil record, as sparse as it is, proves anything, it is that primates can reach the reported size of Bigfoot. The natural environment definitely could support Bigfoot. In fact, Bigfoot's large size here would be a survival advantage, not a disadvantage.

If Bigfoot is real, why didn't people talk about it much before 1958, the year in which casts of its footprints attracted worldwide media attention? Actually, there were accounts of human encounters with Bigfoot, even if the creature didn't yet have that name, long before 1958, when photos of huge footprints cast by a construction crew building a road in a remote section of northern California made Bigfoot an object of worldwide interest.

Native American legends about Sasquatch used to be dismissed largely on the grounds that they were legends. But these same traditional stories include descriptions of bears, mountain lions, and whales, all of which certainly are real. In 1893, future president Theodore Roosevelt published a book, *Wilderness Hunter*, in which he told about his guide's encounter with a Bigfoot-like animal. Roosevelt evidently accepted the guide's account as the truth.

If we can't visit it in a zoo, aquarium, or museum, does that mean it exists only in legend? Have we fully documented every other living creature on the planet, at least those larger than insects? It is arrogant to assume so. It was only in 1992 that the Saola, a hoofed mammal related to rhinos and pigs, was discovered in Vietnam, where it had lived among dense human populations for millennia before being scientifically documented. It is only in recent years that science has recognized that giant squid—the stuff of sailors' wild tales for centuries—are quite real, huge, and difficult to document because of their deep-sea habitat and high intelligence that allows them to evade people.

All of this suggests that Bigfoot could exist, while it does not prove that Bigfoot does exist. Clearly, this calls for an open mind concerning the Pacific Northwest's most mysterious creature. Bigfoot is just one of the many strange beings that you will encounter in this look at the dark side of Washington. Your supernatural tour of the state will take you across both space and time, so prepare for the fearsome, the guilty, and the evil, as well as the welcoming, the innocent, and the benign. Turn on all the lights and settle into a comfortable chair and enjoy, at second hand, tales of terror, suspense, and wonder.

Puget Sound Metropolitan Region

THE PUGET SOUND METROPOLITAN REGION CONTAINS MORE THAN HALF of the state's population. From Marysville and Everett on the north to Olympia in the south, this region seems like a huge interconnected series of cities, towns, and suburbs, all focused on Puget Sound, squeezed between that body of water and the foothills of the Cascades.

On your journey through the supernatural side of this crowded, cosmopolitan region, you'll encounter the spirits of Chief Seattle and his eldest child, Princess Angeline. You'll visit a classic haunted house, along with several haunted theaters. A possible portal to hell is on the tour, as is a truly gruesome, decapitated ghost. You'll learn how ancient traditions and rituals can help a deceased loved one safely move on to the next world. The ghosts of an Indian massacre will haunt you, as will the shades of mistreated mental patients from the past. You'll meet the pathetic ghost of an early victim of one of America's most infamous serial killers, and be reminded of Seattle and Tacoma's early years in several tales of the supernatural.

The Phantom Princess

Quite a few people claim to have seen her, most often at Pike Place Market in Seattle. Her name and image have become famous as an icon of the city—she is quite literally a princess of Seattle.

She certainly is a ghost, for she died more than a century ago on May 31, 1896. A longtime fixture of downtown, she technically was an illegal resident of the city, as all Duwamish Indians were banished to reservations by the 1855 Treaty of Ellicott Point. But Princess Angeline, as she was known to whites, enjoyed the respect, even affection, of her Seattle neighbors because of who she was and what she did.

Princess Angeline was the first child of the great Chief Seattle, for whom the city was named. She really was not a princess because her tribe did not have hereditary chiefs. Although Seattle was the son of a chief, he earned his own chief status through his leadership qualities. He was a courageous warrior, a superb organizer, and a memorable orator, but he is best remembered as a diplomat who preferred negotiations to wars. His tombstone epitaph states that he was a "firm friend of the whites." He warned the whites of any trouble pending and worked to avoid conflict. Princess Angeline herself once paddled her canoe across Puget Sound to warn whites of a planned attack.

Princess Angeline's ghost takes the form of an elderly Native American woman. She usually is reported as wearing a bright red kerchief on her head and an old shawl draped about her shoulders. When Angeline is spotted on the edge of Pike Place Market, she is seated on an old blanket spread on the sidewalk, often near flower stands. She has a variety of handmade baskets, which she offers for sale. The old lady smiles and beckons tourists with a friendly wave, but as they approach her, she simply vanishes, baskets and all. It is not uncommon for confused shoppers to ask nearby merchants what happened to the basket seller. "Oh, that's Princess Angeline," is the reply. "You've just seen a figure from Seattle's past."

Angeline lived in a shack at the foot of Pike Street. She supported herself by taking in laundry as well as making and selling baskets. In life, and now as a ghost, she often is accompanied by a cat and a small dog. Allegedly, as she walked along the streets, she would approach smokers and ask for a light. As the person produced a

match, Angeline would coyly ask, "And would you be able to spare a cigarette?" Her bold smile would usually win a cigarette from passersby, amused by their encounter with a well-known legend of old Seattle. According to some, Angeline's spirit still strolls downtown streets, although she seems to have given up smoking.

Angeline died on May 31, 1896, and was given a lavish funeral at the Church of Our Lady of Good Hope. Her coffin was carved in the shape of a canoe and she was buried among other notable pioneers of Seattle in a hilltop grave. It is local legend that both her dog and cat mourned at her graveside for three days before disappearing.

Other Native American ghosts haunt the city and its environs. Chief Seattle is said to have predicted, "These shores will swarm with the invisible dead of my tribe." Maybe if you're lucky, you'll see these shadows of the past.

His Spirit Marches On

His compelling coal-black eyes are what most people remember best. They flash with intelligence and determination. He is most often glimpsed at the tail end of protest marches, or standing at the back of an auditorium or outdoor rally. Oddly, most of those who claim to have seen him can remember little else about him other than the seamed, leathery brown skin of his determined-looking face and the laserlike intensity of his prominent eyes.

The certainty of having seen him, however briefly, is accompanied by unanswered questions. Who is he? What was he doing at the protest? Some speculate that the "Marching Spirit," as he has been termed, is the ghost of none other than Chief Seattle.

The best clues to this phantom's true identity may lie in his choice of causes to support. This particular shade is never known to attend meetings on behalf of local candidates for office. The ghostly activist seems passionate about two concerns: civil rights for all Americans and environmental conservation.

Chief Seattle was born around 1780. As a small boy, he claimed to have witnessed Capt. George Vancouver's ships exploring Puget Sound in 1792, the first recorded Europeans to do so. When waves of white settlers put irresistible pressure on Seattle's people, he counseled peaceful negotiations as an alternative to wars, which he believed would be a disaster for the Native Americans. On the day after Christmas in 1854, the Medicine Creek Treaty was signed between the United States and the tribes of the Puget Sound area. At the presentation ceremony for the treaty, Seattle is said to have given a magnificent oration in a voice that could be heard several city blocks away. Of this speech, only fragmentary notes made by a white listener survive, but the theme was "a world turned upside down." The respected chief is reported to have observed that the coming of Europeans had totally changed life as his tribe had known it. Flexibility in thinking, adaptability, and mutual respect between Indians and whites would be the keys to survival and a peaceful and prosperous future for all. This line of reasoning by the living man is continued by his spirit's watchful attendance at civil rights demonstrations into the present.

It is not coincidence that when the chief converted to Christianity, he chose the baptism name Noah. Like the Biblical figure, Noah Seattle was deeply concerned with preserving all of God's creatures from oblivion. While the original Noah had to contend with the Great Flood, the new Noah saw the dangers of ruthless exploitation of the forests and fisheries whose bountiful resources had sustained his people for millennia without the negative environmental consequences faced by the mid-nineteenth century Americans. Rallies to save the whales, save the wild salmon, or save the trees always seem to attract the spiritual participation of Chief Seattle.

A few claim to have sensed the spirit of the chief near his gravesite. Seattle died on June 7, 1866, and is buried in Suquamish Memorial Cemetery. A contemplative visit to his grave might inspire a determination to follow Noah's concern to preserve all of creation into the future.

Afraid of Their Shadows

Most of the time, they are seen only as misty shadows, running for their lives, their faces contorted with fear and physical exhaustion. If these supernatural shadows persist long enough, the source of their panicked flight is revealed—a band of Puyallup Indians in hot pursuit, brandishing clubs and tomahawks. Some of those who claim to have witnessed this spectral attack believe that they've seen the whites brutally clubbed and hacked to death. Others swear that they saw the marauding Indians scalping their luckless victims, producing corpses literally drenched in blood.

These nightmarish visions allegedly represent a recurring, ghostly reenactment of the infamous White River Massacre, a gruesome incident in the Indian wars of the 1850s that occurred in what is now Washington State. The White River Massacre, in which nine members of three pioneer families were killed on October 28, 1855, was especially tragic in that it could have been avoided. Perhaps it is this very avoidability that motivates the spirits of the massacre's victims to reenact their final agonies around the anniversary of their deaths.

The whole year had been tense throughout the territory. Some tribes, like the Duwamish, led by Chief Seattle, were agreeable to peaceful negotiations, while others clearly were restive. In early October, a local man, Allen Porter, rode down the White River Valley, Paul Revere-style, warning the settlers of a probable Indian attack. He had seen war parties of young braves on the move and heard rumors of a war to exterminate the white settlers who were seen as encroaching on traditional tribal lands and threatening the continuation of Indian culture. Most whites in the neighborhood took the warning very seriously and fled with their families to the relative security of the stockade at Seattle, about twenty-five miles away. Soldiers were sent to the abandoned farms to investigate that threat. The heavily armed soldiers were received peacefully by the Puyallup, who reassured the soldiers of their peaceful intentions, which was reported naively back to Seattle.

"You are afraid of your own shadows," the smirking soldiers told the panicked settlers. "You are seeing monsters under your beds like little kids." Reluctantly, the settlers returned to their vulnerably isolated farmsteads and there paid the price for others' misplaced optimism and complacency. Accused of cowardice, they have now become shadows themselves—shadows of violent and needless death. Incidentally, the community of Auburn was first named Slaughter, after an army lieutenant, William Slaughter, who was killed by Indians soon after the White River Massacre. The double meaning made it an appropriate name, but business-minded civic leaders thought that the name Auburn would attract more settlers to the scene of the infamous and unnecessary White River Massacre. Alas, those shadows of the murdered settlers keep showing up.

A Classic Haunted House

Lakewood's Thornewood Castle not only looks as though it's haunted, it is haunted, at least according to some. As guests approach the magnificently restored house, the largest American castle still in private hands, they often do a double take. It is their first sight of Thornewood, but it looks so familiar. It is familiar to those who've seen the 2002 TV miniseries *Rose Red*, scripted by the master of horror stories, Stephen King. As those familiar with the miniseries know, the house is not just a backdrop for the story. The house becomes, in effect, the main character in the story, becoming a kind of malignant organism that feeds off the life force of the unfortunate inhabitants. *Rose Red* delivered enough frights to please any fan of Stephen King, but the actual resident ghosts are of a much more benign type, at least according to recent reports.

Thornewood Castle dates to 1911, but many of its building materials and decorative features are much older. Bricks already four centuries old were shipped all the way from an English castle being dismantled. Some of Thornwood's priceless stained glass windows date to the eleventh century. The Gothic Tudor house is filled with period antiques, so that it really does look like it belongs in Elizabethan England. The horror film clichés of dust and cobwebs do not apply to Thornewood, which was thoroughly renovated for its star turn in *Rose Red*.

As a private residence, Thornewood hosted two U.S. presidents—Theodore Roosevelt and William Howard Taft, neither of whom reported seeing ghosts. The fifty-four-room castle is now a luxurious bed-and-breakfast and a favorite venue for wedding receptions and elaborate parties for all occasions.

Thornewood, located in a gated community, is open only to registered guests, not the general public; it cannot even be seen from the road. As befits the luxurious and historic splendor of its guest facilities, Thornewood's ghosts are said to be antique, interesting, and politely behaved.

Among the most frequently seen phantoms are those of the original master and mistress of the castle, Chester and Anna Thorn. Anna's suite often functions as a dressing room for the bride and her attendants. Supposedly, more than one bride has stood before the original full-length mirror to check her appearance, only to see a second figure behind her in the reflection. On turning, of course, no one else is there. It is thought that Anna's spirit, drawn by the spiritual radiance of the bride, has stopped in to give her silent blessing. A glimpse of Anna in her mirror has become common enough to be regarded as good luck.

Chester Thorn's unseen spirit is said to tour the house late at night, turning lights on and off and checking that windows are closed against rain or cold weather. Is Chester, who loved playing the gracious host, still making sure that the house is secure and comfortable?

Less frequently seen or heard ghosts allegedly include servants in medieval costume. Perhaps some very old spirits have come all the way from England with the bricks, stained glass windows, and furniture. These shades of servants have been known to curtsy or bow to guests before simply disappearing. Their ephemeral appearances are intriguing but never scary. In a strange but unthreatening way, they are an interesting complement to the many amenities the historic castle has to offer the pampered guests. Even if no ghosts show up, a visit to Thornewood Castle is a rewarding and enjoyable experience.

The Haunted Theater

It is not unusual for theaters to be haunted. Spiritualists believe that this is because of the very high intensities of psychic energy expended by actors and actresses as they replicate strong emotions on stage. Tacoma's Pantages Theater, built in 1918 by noted impresario Alexander Pantages, is famously haunted. This opulent theater, modeled on the royal theater at the palace of Versailles in France, was lavishly restored in 1983. The Pantages stays busy as the home of Tacoma's civic opera, ballet, and orchestra, all of which seem to be enjoyed by the theater's resident ghosts.

The most self-effacing phantom is that of a middle-aged gentleman, dressed immaculately in tuxedo, white shirt, black tie, and fresh red rose in his buttonhole. He has been spotted repeatedly in the orchestra section, shifting back and forth among the seats as though checking them for comfort and sightings to the stage. He appears to be anxious about something, his eyes darting nervously about as he shifts positions. When he senses living eyes on him, he vanishes. No one is sure what his background and motivation might be.

Another frequently seen spirit is that of an elderly cleaning woman who shows up as the theater empties after a performance. Bent with age and fatigue, she methodically pushes an old-fashioned carpet sweeper up and down the aisles, apparently oblivious to the fact that her efforts do not succeed in removing any dirt or debris.

As reported by at least one young actress, the most glamorous ghost could be that of a legendary sex goddess. Mae West's phantom is alleged to appear specifically to mentor young actresses just beginning their show business careers, especially those suffering from bad cases of stage fright. It is known that Mae West appeared at the Pantages on several occasions.

As recounted by one young, awestruck actress, Mae materialized backstage on opening night of a Broadway musical revival. A buxom, middle-aged woman, dressed in a smock like those worn by dressers and makeup artists, suddenly appeared at the side of the young woman. "Relax, kiddo," advised the heavily made-up woman, batting huge artificial eyelashes under her platinum blonde wig. "The audience is here to have a good time. They'll love you if you just give them a wink and a smile." Opening night went well, and the beginner was personally visited in the dressing room by her volunteer counselor, offering her the "tricks of the trade" as she put it. "Delay your entrance on stage by just a second or two," she advised. "The other actors will turn to look your way, and the audience's eyes will follow their gaze—it makes for an effective entrance." Some of the unsolicited advice was considerably earthier, as it concerned exaggerated swinging of the hips and outthrust bosom.

It was only later, when the young actress saw a photo of Mae West in her prime, that she realized she'd been visited by one of the most famous stage and screen personalities of the 1920s and '30s. Mae was a self-styled sexpot who made a career out of mocking American's hypocritical pretensions about their private interest in sexuality and public stance on morality in popular culture. Although she cultivated a public image of rampant sexuality, it was mostly talk, literally. Mae wrote her own plays and her own screen dialogue, which emphasized double-meanings and innuendo, but carefully skirted real obscenity. Her famous tagline, "Come on up and see me sometime," was delivered to costar Cary Grant in 1933's *She Done Him Wrong*, a classic comedy that made her one of the highest paid stars of the 1930s.

Incredibly Mae was still doing her "sex bomb" act in her seventies, producing a popular Las Vegas revue in which she appeared surrounded by handsome bodybuilders. One of the young actresses supposedly mentored by Mae's spirit told of being guided about the stage by Mae's unseen hands at her back, eerily reminiscent of Mae's own experience while filming her last movie, *Sextette*, in 1978, when she was eighty-five years old. Nearly blind, Mae was shown from the waist up only, because she was being guided around the sets by an assistant crouching behind her.

So far, Mae West's ghost has only revealed itself to neophyte actresses—but you never know, she did love being on stage. Watch carefully at the Pantages Theater.

Mystery of the Theater Ghost

The central question for true believers and skeptics alike is "Are there really ghosts?" Most of those who've had some sort of encounter steadfastly repeat their belief that it was a genuine experience, not the product of an overactive imagination or a mind clouded by drugs or alcohol.

Then there is the problem of pranks. Some public revelations result in deliberate attempts to make people think a place is haunted. Such is the strange case of the Harvard Exit Theater in Seattle.

As recorded in Rosemary Ellen Guiley's *Encyclopedia of Ghosts and Spirits*, this cinema was said to be haunted in the 1970s through the mid 1980s. The haunting, if that is what it was, seems to have ceased by the late 1980s. There is some conflicting evidence and a decidedly mixed group of opinions as to what really happened. The Harvard Exit Theater, named after a freeway exit, occupied part of an old building on Capitol Hill. The three-story building, constructed in 1925, also housed the Woman's Century Club, originally a suffragist movement that is now a civic organization. The main auditorium is on the second floor, and a second auditorium was later added to the third floor. The third floor was the locale of most of the supposed hauntings.

The first manager of the Harvard Exit Theater saw a woman, dressed in the style of the early twentieth century, sitting near a fireplace. As the manager approached, the figure became misty and then disappeared. Mysterious footsteps and doors slamming by themselves increased a sense of something strange going on.

The manager shared these experiences with other staff, after which the alleged haunting seemed to escalate. He arrived first in the morning, finding lights already on and chairs rearranged in a circle near the fireplace. A projector was found running in the projection booth. The apparition of the woman appeared and disappeared with some regularity. This ghost was tentatively identified as that of Bertha Landes, an early leader of the women's suffrage movement, who led the Woman's Century Club and was Seattle's first woman mayor. She was a noted reformer who died in 1943.

The theater's second manager had such unnerving experiences that he swore never to be alone again in the building. Later, some staff admitted to secretly turning on lights and rearranging furniture, but strongly denied anything to do with the apparitions. They had decided to exploit their boss's fears with these pranks; they assumed, however, that the ghost's appearances really happened. The alleged paranormal activity at the Harvard Exit Theater ceased when the building's small collection of Bertha Landes memorabilia was relocated to a new museum.

Did Mayor Landes's spirit move to the new museum to be with her personal possessions? Workmen building the new museum noted mysteriously missing tools and rearranged furniture, but did not report any visual apparitions, unlike the "floating ball of light" documented by a group of ghost hunters who surveyed the theater back in 1985.

Could the theater ghost have been a genuine haunting, complicated by an overlay of jokes played by some of the living? Perhaps we'll never know now.

The Decapitated Ghost

The Decapitated Ghost appears at Ebey's Landing National Historic Reserve less frequently than in the past; this uniquely macabre entity is said to now materialize only on moonlit nights. Some local Native American groups believed that the full moon somehow summoned forth the dead, especially those restless spirits who were the victims of violence. As it so happened, many Europeans had the same traditions of the full moon's supernatural powers and influences. If you do see this very frightening apparition, you'll know it is Col. Isaac Ebey's ghost by the way he carries his head—tucked under his arm.

Colonel Ebey was an important figure in Washington's early history. He was instrumental in helping to found the future state capital, the city of Olympia. The colonel settled at Ebey's Landing in 1850; his land claim was about forty miles south of the town of Coupeville on scenic Whidbey Island.

Although the native peoples of the Pacific coast—known as the Canoe Indians to early settlers—were less violent in reacting to the arrival of whites than the tribes to the east of the Cascades (the so-called Horse Indians), they still raided numerous white settlements in the 1850s. One dark night in 1857, a band of Haida Indians from British Columbia knocked on Colonel Ebey's door, awakening his family. The colonel himself answered it. The rest of the family heard voices raised in anger, followed by a blood-curdling scream, then an ominous silence. The family fled in panic, jumping out windows and running into the woods. At daybreak, they crept back to the house and found Ebey's bloody corpse—minus his head. The Haida had decapitated him and taken his head as a trophy.

Ebey's headless body was then buried. His family members reported nightly repetitions of the same, deeply disturbing nightmare. The ghostly image of the severed head appeared to them, pleading to be reunited with the body in the grave. Isaac's spirit could not rest until his head and body laid together.

Although Ebey's attackers were never apprehended, the missing head was handed to Capt. Charles Dodd of the Hudson's Bay Company many years later. Dodd knew the whole story of the decapitation and returned the head to the Ebey family. The head was duly buried with the rest of the corpse. Ever afterward, Isaac Ebey's

ghost has been spotted walking along the bluffs above his landing, carrying his head under his arm, as it will not stay on his shoulders. In daylight, tourists climb that bluff to admire the distant view of the Olympic Mountains to the west. On moonlit nights, the ghost walks there, so the site is best avoided by those who would be unnerved by the unusual apparition. Some claim that the head's eyelids suddenly snap open and bright red eyes glare out at the living. Perhaps fans of horror films would actually prefer a moonlit stroll near the small stone monument marking the site of this long-ago atrocity.

Thirteen Steps to Hell

Don't bother looking for them. They cannot be seen by anyone now, and that is very good news for the curious. Descending the legendary thirteen steps could be a truly harrowing experience, or so the stories claim. The thirteen steps led down to the entrance of an elaborate tomb. They also led to a paralyzing, horrific view of hell.

The descending stone staircase has been obliterated from view by bulldozing earth over the stairs and the tomb. This act of mercy occurred more than two decades ago at the cemetery in the tiny community of Maltby. Unauthorized digging in the cemetery would not only be disrespectful and illegal, it would likely be dangerous to the life and sanity of the diggers. Pity the archeologists of some far future time who might accidentally uncover the infamous thirteen steps; the least of the consequences of doing so would be a lifetime of terrible nightmares.

The mausoleums built by the wealthy to receive the coffins of family members are usually above ground, looking like small scale temples or churches. But one was built below ground, reached by thirteen steps. Why? Local legend holds that this was the express command of the deceased, as written in his will. This prominent citizen, who died in 1910, had made a fabulous fortune in the timber business. In the late nineteenth century, this was a rapacious activity in general, and this man's business ethics and personal behavior plumbed new depths of environmental destruction and worker exploitation. No thought was given to managing the forest as a sustainable resource. No consideration was given to worker safety in a notoriously dangerous occupation.

One day a falling tree killed a logger and seriously injured another. A spinal injury crippled the latter below the waist. In an instant he was transformed from a young, vigorous logger into a severely handicapped, wheelchair-bound man who could never work again in the forests. He begged his boss for an office job, something that would enable him to make a living. "No, absolutely not" was the answer, "I don't want to look at a pathetic cripple in my office every day!"

"But I'll have to beg on the streets," pleaded the ex-logger.

"Good idea!" said the callous boss, "Here's your first nickel." He laughed as he tossed a coin at his former employee.

"Damn you to hell!" shouted the scorned man.

The object of his curse simply laughed. "I'm already destined for hell—the Devil is my partner."

Whether this was meant literally or not, the wealthy man's will specified a belowground mausoleum. "All the better to be close to hell," as he wrote. Did he actually create a portal to hell? It is said that, a few days after the funeral, the deceased's oldest son descended the thirteen steps to pay his respects. He was then heard to scream in terror before passing out. Three days later, he committed suicide and became the tomb's second occupant. No family members ever again visited the tomb.

Years later, two children, curious about the staircase, approached the door to the tomb. They were found comatose at the foot of the stairs. Their eyebrows and hair were singed as though from close contact with a flame. The children never spoke again, only whimpered uncontrollably. They died in an insane asylum.

For decades, rumors of tortured screams coming from the vicinity of the thirteen steps gave the cemetery an evil reputation. Finally, the decision was made to bury the staircase and its tomb entrance under a mound of earth. This closed the portal, but are there others? Only the Devil knows.

Shade of a Pioneer

The distinguished old gentleman was decked out in stylish late-Victorian fashion. He was wearing a three-piece dark suit. The rather gaudy vest was embroidered with gold thread, setting off the vibrant gold and midnight-blue silk tie. The long white beard enhanced his astonishingly close resemblance to the famous pioneer who had built the mansion and whose photo was prominently displayed in the front parlor. Apparently pleased that the visitors took notice of him, the man smiled and began descending the elaborately carved staircase. The visitors turned away to summon their friends to share the moment. One snapped a quick picture of the old gentleman as a souvenir of their memorable wedding reception at the Meeker Mansion in Puyallup, complete with an impersonator of Ezra Meeker himself, posed as the gracious host.

When the reception guests returned their gazes to the staircase, however, "Ezra" had disappeared. Later, one guest complimented the banquet manager on arranging for an impersonator in period costume to remind everyone of the historical significance of the house.

"What impersonator?" was the reply. "We don't have an impersonator here today."

"Then just who did we see on the stairs?" the guest asked.

The staff could only shrug their shoulders. Had old Ezra Meeker's spirit somehow materialized at his beloved home?

Ezra Meeker crowded many accomplishments into his ninety-seven years on earth. He crossed half a continent in an oxcart, helping to pioneer the famous Oregon Trail that brought many early settlers to the Pacific Northwest. He founded the town of Puyallup in 1862 and served as its first mayor. Beer drinkers salute him, perhaps unknowingly, every time they hoist a brew. Meeker introduced the growing of hops into the region, and hops made him rich. He took his wife, Eliza Jane, along on a sales trip to England, where they met Queen Victoria. Mrs. Meeker was awed by the queen's lifestyle and decided that her husband could afford a much nicer abode. Her dream house, finished in 1890, took three years to complete. It is in this mansion that people still sense Ezra's spirit.

Ezra Meeker was determined that the Oregon Trail and its role in settling the northwestern frontier should never be forgotten. He wrote a novel and children's book about his adventures along the trail and started a national campaign to preserve and mark the trail's most important places. He traveled the old trail by oxcart a second time in 1910, followed by an automotive trip in 1916. The car was fitted with a prairie schooner canvas top. In 1924, at the age of ninety-four, Ezra flew along the same route in an open-cockpit plane. His genius for publicity did result in official recognition of the Oregon Trail. It is believed that his phantom appears regularly at historical markers along the trail. Of course it is easier and more likely to see his spirit in the luxurious comfort of his beloved mansion.

If you should catch a quick glimpse of Ezra Meeker's spirit, it might be appropriate to toast his memory with a tall, cold glass of beer, enjoying the taste and aroma of hops.

Better Listen to Granny

The family in this story wishes to remain unidentified; we'll call them the Rileys. The Rileys have lived in Seattle for three generations now, but their heritage is Irish and Scotch. Recently, they've come to a new appreciation and respect for ancient Celtic customs concerning death.

The dreams, which many family members seemed to share, started on the very night that Uncle Pat died. His fatal heart attack took everyone by surprise, including his doctor. The emergency medical team rushed him to the hospital, but it was much too late.

In the first round of common dreams afflicting family members, Pat, who normally was a life-of-the-party type, appeared to be confused, wandering about aimlessly and with a morose, unblinking stare, as though lost. As Pat had been proud of his Irish and Scotch heritage, with all its folklore and customs, the family decided that he would have appreciated their having an old-fashioned wake the night before his burial. It was a disaster. Light bulbs exploded as they were turned on, doors slammed at random, and small objects flew off tables and shattered on the floor. And, horror of horrors, a half-full bottle of good Irish whiskey, bought for the occasion, somehow got smashed in the sink. When a small child innocently asked where Uncle Pat had gone, a howling wind suddenly sprang up and blew in the front door. There was some nervous joking about Pat not wanting to miss a party, and then the gathering quickly broke up.

That night, many family members had a common dream with Pat as the central figure. This time he appeared both confused and angry. Why was Pat's spirit so upset? The answer was provided the next day at the luncheon following the trip to the cemetery. Old

Granny O'Brien, who normally resided in a distant nursing home, overheard tales of the dreams and the unsettling wake. It was clear to Granny, if not to everyone else, that the fault lay with Pat's family. They had not honored the old ways, and their negligence had confused and disheartened Pat. Granny began to list what they must do in order to help Pat move on to the next world. She was quite explicit. Her recollection of ancient traditions was much better than her memory of what she'd had for breakfast that morning.

As Pat already was in the grave, they needed to create a substitute for his body and follow the prescribed rituals as though his corpse was present. Old Jewish customs, adopted by Christians, called for lighting candles for the dead and dying. A lit candle would keep away demons and it must remain lit for a week after the burial. Twelve candles must burn in a circle around the recently deceased's body—the circle of fire would prevent evil spirits from taking away the soul. Pat's shoes, wallet, and tweed cap substituted for his body. Following burial, three candles must be burned in the room in which the death occurred. The stubs of these candles should be saved and used to heal any burns or cuts on family members. If any of these candles burns dim, it means a ghost is nearby and appropriate prayers should be read aloud. Granny's instructions were followed to the letter and Pat's family was no longer afflicted by bad dreams. According to Granny, his soul was at peace at last thanks to their practicing the old traditions.

Joining the Party

It was difficult, if not downright impossible, for the tourists to get to sleep that night, despite being exhausted from a very busy day of sightseeing. The tourists, a middle-aged couple from New Jersey, were making their first visit to Seattle. It was a second honeymoon trip, a kind of celebration that their youngest had just gone off to college, leaving them, at least temporarily, with an empty nest. The couple's carefully saved frequent-flier miles would stretch to Seattle, so why not?

A friend of a friend had recommended the Hotel Andra as a reasonably priced, very comfortable place convenient to the monorail and Pike Place Market. Older structures like the Andra, formerly the Claremont, usually had thick walls that reduced the problem of noisy neighbors, or so the visitors hoped. They had booked a three-night stay and looked forward to blissful sleep. They would be disappointed.

The sounds began at midnight, when most noisy parties are beginning to wind down. It sounded like either a live combo or a very fine sound system. The music was distinctively 1920s style, featuring lots of piano and saxophone. Early Cole Porter was the tourists' conclusion—bouncy rhythms and sophisticated lyrics that indicated good musical taste, along with a certain insensitivity to others trying to sleep. Phone complaints to the front desk, answered by a groggy night clerk, resulted in sympathy but no action. "We haven't had any other complaints," as though that excused the culprits.

The riotous party seemed to be directly overhead. The tourists decided on bold action. They would dress, go upstairs, and confront the partiers. Maybe their personal pleas would succeed in lowering the volume. Or, as the husband secretly hoped, maybe they'd be invited to join what sounded like a lively good time.

Persistent knocking finally brought a man to the door. He looked drunk and very happy. "Oh, I'm sorry about the noise," he said. "We'll try to keep it down. Say, how would you folks like to join us for a drink?"

It didn't take too much persuasion. The music was lively and the food and liquor were of the best quality. The other partygoers were dressed in 1920s high style—tuxedoes for the gentlemen and ladies decked out in glittering short skirts and lots of beads. "Is this a costume party?" queried the New Jerseyian. His question was met with a lot of good-natured laughter. "No, we thought you folks were in costume!" was the drunken reply.

As dawn approached, the couple fell fast asleep on a couch in the spacious suite. They were awakened by a very puzzled chambermaid. "You are not supposed to be in here—no one should be here. I've come to freshen up for guests tonight."

The maid checked their room keys and admonished them that they were on the wrong floor and in an executive suite. The couple explained being disturbed by the sounds of a loud party and how they joined the party. "But no one could have been in here last night," claimed the maid. "Look around—the room is clean and undisturbed, and your key could not have opened this door."

"Yes, our key wouldn't fit, but here we are," observed the wife, becoming a little agitated. Back in their own room, the couple finally noticed, gratefully, that despite a memory of heavy drinking, they had no hangovers. Good luck, good booze, or a result of just a dream?

Despite recurring sounds of merriment from the floor above, the couple stayed in their own room that evening. Wouldn't you?

"Oh, the Blood!"

"Oh, the blood! The blood!" The words are spoken in a breathy whisper. But were they words or just the wind outside? It is difficult to be certain. Some claim that the whispers say, "No, the blood! No!" While there are disagreements on the exact words, there seems to be an awed consensus on the apparition that is believed to be voicing them. The misty, almost transparent form is that of a handsome, middle-aged gentleman. His face is contorted in an expression that is at once sad and terrified. His red eyes seem to focus on an astonishing sight just inches in front of him at waist level. An old-fashioned heavy china washbowl appears to float in the air, preceding the phantom as he walks slowly down the hall, approaching the elaborate staircase. "Oh, the blood!" he moans, or is it just the old timbers of the house responding to the pressure of the wind?

Relatively few have encountered this pitiable, though scary, ghost. Perhaps his psychic energy gradually is draining from the house, the scene of a monstrous crime the living man may have perpetrated. Or was it truly an accident? Probably, this terrible incident may never be fully resolved. Maybe it never happened at all— legends are not always based on facts.

According to the old story, the haunting takes place in the old manor house at Woodville's well-known Chateau Ste. Michelle Winery. The wines are justifiably famous; the story behind the ghost less so.

The manor house is an early 1900s mansion and was built by lumber baron Fred Stimson. He enjoyed his vast wealth, as his beautiful house demonstrates. Allegedly, his appreciation of beauty extended to a young, pretty housemaid named Elizabeth. Elizabeth became pregnant, which horrified Fred.

Shortly after, Elizabeth fell down the mansion stairs, broke her neck, and died, along with the child she was carrying. Was it really just an accident? We'll never know for sure. The legend of the manor house ghost, however, seems to support the possibility that it was no accident.

The anguished ghost is trying to wash his hands in the bowl that appears to hover in the air in front of him. His hands drip blood, which he cannot wash off. The bowl itself, according to some, is filled with blood. Is the blood that cannot be washed away symbolic of guilt that cannot be washed off unrepentant hands?

This particular spirit has not been reported much recently. Perhaps this lost soul has at last moved on to the spirit world.

The Starving Ghosts

The words are heard only faintly and almost seem to blend in with the sounds of the wind coming off the Sinclair Inlet. The reaction of many of those who've heard the pitiful, barely perceptible pleas for food and mercy is to question their own senses. Did they really hear those moaning entreaties or was it just a combination of the wind with their imaginations?

"Food, please—bread, anything—I'm so hungry! Have mercy!" Variations on these themes seem to be repeated endlessly, ranging from heart-wrenching shouts to whimpering whispers. As the wind blows harder, the pleas increase in volume, and then they diminish to breathy moans. Sometimes, though not always, the sounds are accompanied by slightly phosphorescent forms. These sad apparitions seem to be unusually gaunt in appearance, with only thin veneers of flesh over their bones.

Encounters with the starving ghosts of Port Orchard can be profoundly disturbing to those who experience them. The starving ghosts are far more pathetic than they are frightening. After an instinctive recoil at a supernatural confrontation, the next reaction generally is one of sympathy. After all, one trait that identifies us as truly human is our instinctive impulse to share food. We hate to see anyone go hungry. Most people willingly share food; most animals do not. Even temporary hunger pangs focus our thoughts on obtaining food. Chronic hunger would be an unrelenting spur to sustain life. Literally starving to death could, quite understandably, produce some memorably pitiful ghosts.

The starving ghosts of Port Orchard are the results of an agonizingly horrific experiment performed upon helpless, hopeless victims of mental illness.

About a century ago, a small, local insane asylum was headed by a ruthless and evil doctor, Linda Burfield Hazzard. Dr. Hazzard developed a frighteningly exploitive theory of treating mental illness. She asserted that most psychoses were the result of chemical imbalances in the brain. These, she claimed, were by-products of toxic contaminants in food. She advocated cleansing the body of food-related substances by withholding food until the patient's mental state improved. Conveniently, this lowered the costs of patient care. Dr. Hazzard was able to produce wills signed by deceased inmates of her gruesome institution leaving all their assets to her. As no one ever recovered their sanity under this treatment, Dr. Hazzard grew rich and the number of unmarked graves on her property multiplied. Allegedly, when she ran out of gravesites, she simply tossed the corpses of her victims over the cliff and into the sea.

And so, the spirits of the wretched victims of starvation periodically beg for food, the denial of which led to their untimely deaths.

Phantoms of Skid Road

First of all, the original term was *skid road*, not skid row. The "row" part was a result of a journalist's typo. Skid roads in American cities are those areas on the edge of downtowns where the poorest of the poor congregate. The name originated in the logging industry and came to be applied to city streets where loggers gathered for a drink or two and often a lot more. In the old days, loggers were a poorly paid, rough-and-tumble lot. Urban skid roads had a reputation for seedy bars, drunken brawls, and unsavory activities.

Seattle's Yesler Way was a real skid road about a hundred and thirty years ago. Pioneer loggers used to clear a crude path through the forest. The enormous logs, which were cut on the western slopes of the Cascades, could not be handled by sleighs or wagons. The ground was too rough and the soil was too soft, so trees were felled across the crude paths at right angles, like railroad ties. These trees, or "skids," were lubricated with grease. Teams of oxen then dragged great logs over the skids.

Yesler Way was a skid road bringing logs to Yesler's Mill. Loggers were kept "south of the line," or Yesler Way, to avoid contact with respectable folk north of the road. The Pioneer Square area, especially South Washington and South Main Streets, became the loggers' playground, the place where dreams died amid poverty and alcoholism.

Pioneer Square has changed. It now boasts trendy restaurants, popular bars, and glittering nightlife, far from its onetime low reputation. But the ghosts of the loggers still walk these streets, and it would be a good idea to stay out of their way.

The phantom loggers seem solid enough at first—with solid muscle from the incredibly hard work they performed for ten hours a day, six days a week. These spirits are deeply under the influence of the kind of spirits that come in bottles. Some are benignly happy drunks; some are mean, frustrated drunks. Don't look them in the eye; just keep walking. With a bit of luck, the ghost loggers will simply evaporate before you really panic. They can't physically harm you, but they surely can put a scare into you.

In the heyday of the real skid roads, the loggers were known as "timber beasts" and were both scorned and feared by most of their fellow citizens. Their work was hard and dangerous and their pay was a pathetic two dollars a day. They typically drank and played as hard as they worked. The bars at the ends of skid roads were notorious for heavy drinking, violent fights, rough play, and rougher language. Genteel folks stayed well clear of the timber beasts.

Enjoy Pioneer Square, but don't go for a solitary stroll after the bars close. You don't want to meet the phantoms of the skid road gone by.

The Holland Road Phantom

As the man later admitted, he was driving a little too fast, but he swore that he was not drunk or under the influence of drugs. He said he did not imagine seeing the girl on the horse, the sight that caused him to swerve into the roadside tree. The veteran police officer investigating the one-vehicle accident nodded sympathetically.

"Yes, I know that you really saw her, but I also know she wasn't really there." Like many people before him, the unfortunate driver had witnessed the phantom of Holland Road in Bremerton.

The phantom dates back to 1937, when a tragic car crash ended the earthly existence of a twelve-year-old girl. The story, according to old-timers in the area, is that an accidental homicide was covered up to protect the reputation of a wealthy businessman and keep him out of jail. Justice was thwarted, at least for the living. Justice triumphed, however, in the world of spirits.

Unquestionably, the man was drunk—blind drunk as they used to say. He'd been celebrating yet another business coup, driving a characteristically sharp bargain at the expense of a less ruthless competitor. The man's business dealings bordered on fraud, not that that kept him awake at night. Too high a speed and too many martinis, combined with a foggy evening, led to disaster. The girl on horseback seemed to materialize out of the fog. It was too late to avoid her. The girl was thrown from her horse and under the wheels of the heavy car, killing her instantly.

Sobered by a surge of adrenaline, the man reacted quickly. Fortunately for him, it was a lonely stretch of road with no other traffic. He hustled to his home nearby and began making frantic phone calls. Friends and loyal employees soon arrived. The little victim was buried hastily in a nearby field owned by the culprit. The heavily damaged car was towed to a car dealership owned by the shameless drunk and dismantled overnight. The girl's horse was led to a meatpacking plant owned by a business associate and became an unusual ingredient in sausage. All traces of the event were thus erased.

His victim in an unmarked, unconsecrated grave, the man relaxed. No one could touch him now, or so he thought.

One week after the accident, the man choked to death during a breakfast of sausage and eggs. The fresh sausage had been a gift from his friend who owned the packing plant that disposed of the girl's horse. Soon afterward, or so the story goes, the man's wife, who was complicit in the cover-up, shot herself in the head. Her suicide note said that she couldn't stand being haunted by the specter of the dead girl, who visited her every night.

The businessman's house was hastily abandoned by all of its subsequent owners, who fled in panic after encountering a mysterious phantom riding a black horse. The horse and its rider had red, glowing eyes that seemed to bore right into their souls.

It is said that, to this day, drivers on that section of Holland Road still glimpse a girl on horseback in the road, especially if they are exceeding the speed limit. So slow down on Holland Road, and on foggy nights, find an alternate route.

Tortured Whispers

"No, no. Please, no, not again. Not anymore. No." These pleading, hopeless words are spoken in a husky, breathy voice just above a whisper. Those who hear it, horrified by the content, are never really sure that they've heard it at all. The sound is at the lower edge of a person's hearing range—almost subliminal. Did they really hear it? Was it their imagination playing tricks on them? One person likened it to turning on the mute function on the television late at night, with no competing noises; the speakers still put out a weak, tinny, just barely audible leak of sound. Of course, some people who've lived in the apartment deny hearing anything at all. Perhaps hearing the whimpered pleas for mercy requires some mystical sensitivity to spiritual energy. Some believe that the faint cries are the ghostly echoes of the torture and murder of Lynda Ann Healy, who died there on January 31, 1974.

This sadistic and truly horrifying murder took place in a basement apartment, which will not be identified, near the University of Washington campus to the north of downtown Seattle. The 639-acre campus, famed for its towering trees and lush landscaping, is home to 35,000 students. Among them, in the early 1970s, were several of victims of one of the most notorious and vicious serial killers in American history.

Lynda Ann Healy, whose agonized phantom is said to occasionally haunt the scene of her death, is thought to have been the first victim of Theodore Robert "Ted" Bundy, whose sadistic torture-murders of more than thirty young women are stomach-turning for even the most jaded devotees of horror films. Poor Lynda Ann was a good example of Bundy's taste in victims—a beautiful, slender young woman with long, straight blond hair. What distinguished Ted Bundy as a killer was his twisted obsession with prolonging the agony of his victims as long as possible. He became the demented feline in a sick game of cat and mouse, toying with those he was killing. He killed, not out of greed, rage, jealousy, or unbridled lust, but for the sheer pleasure it provided him. Bundy was a handsome man of above average intelligence, and he was a charmer—a fatal charmer. After almost ten years on death row, he was put to death in Florida's electric chair on January 24, 1989. Completely unrepentant, he refused to help police locate the bodies of victims like Lynda Ann, commenting that, "I'm the most cold-blooded son of a bitch you'll ever meet."

All that was left behind in his first victim's Seattle apartment was a bloody nightgown and bedding. And, of course, Lynda Ann's tortured spirit. And those bone-chilling whispers for mercy, or perhaps merciful death.

The Truly Tortured Spirits

It would be hard to say which has the greater number of ghosts—the hospital or its cemetery. The cemetery contains more than three thousand graves; the old hospital is said to hold countless ghosts—some pathetic, many terrifying.

Mental institutions, especially those dating back to the 1800s, are infamous "hot spots" in the shadowy world of apparitions. They are thought to be repositories of so much negative human emotion and psychic energy that they are virtual warehouses of tortured souls. In the shameful past, their inmates, already in mental torment, also were subjected to physical torture that had been officially sanctioned. Patients needed help, but some medical staff of the distant past sadistically abused their helpless victims. The bad old days are gone but not forgotten. Especially not forgotten by the resident ghosts.

Lakewood's Western State Hospital welcomed—if that's the right phrase—its first patients in 1871. It still functions as a mental health facility, surely the only one in the nation that contains a small museum open by appointment to the public. The museum offers fascinating, if rather disturbing, glimpses into the history of treatments of mental illness. Exhibits are housed in a former ward. By day, the artifacts of straitjackets, electroshock apparatus, and the like can be unsettling, to say the least. At night, the ghosts seem to take over. As one of the museum's founders was quoted in the *Tacoma News Tribune* on August 6, 2006, "The old asylum ward can be creepy at night. The floors creak. Voices echo. The wind whistles eerily through the small hospital windows. Your imagination can take over."

In 1936, the hospital began using insulin shock therapy, where a patient is induced into a coma, then shocked out of it. By 1941, electroshock therapy was in use on schizophrenics. In 1942, lobotomies were introduced, in which nerve fibers connecting the brain's frontal lobes are severed. This procedure was used into the 1960s, but is now outlawed. Those bad old days are behind us now, but the tortured souls who once experienced them are said to still be around. The most glamorous and most pathetic ghost is believed to be that of movie star Frances Farmer.

Frances was born in Seattle in 1913. Her flawless beauty got her a contract with a major Hollywood studio, where she made a handful of not-particularly-memorable films in the 1940s. She was never a star of the first rank, which she blamed on the studio. Frances believed that the studio used her beauty as mere decoration, as "living wallpaper," as she put it, never really exploiting her acting talents. The studio classified her as too temperamental, too difficult to handle. There is little doubt that Farmer was an alcoholic; she was arrested repeatedly for drunk driving and showered arresting officers with verbal abuse. A Los Angeles mental hospital diagnosed her as manic-depressive and used insulin shock therapy. Her studio contract canceled, Frances went to live with her parents in Seattle. She attacked her mother, who placed her in Western State Hospital against her will. Diagnosed as schizophrenic, Frances was subjected to electroshock therapy over a period of five years from 1945 to 1950. A biography of Frances, *Shadowland*, recounted years of terrible abuse in the hospital, a charge denied by Western State officials.

Frances Farmer's spirit, it is said, still roams the old ward now converted to a museum. Her lovely face contorted by a blend of pain and rage, hers is both a frightening and pathetic ghost. The unique museum is well worth a visit—just don't linger about as night approaches and phantoms roam.

Tacoma's Colorful Spirits

Tacoma had a colorful start. It was in every sense a town of the Wild West. Unlike the storied towns of the southwest, Tacoma was not a frontier mining town. It was a different kind of frontier—one based on the timber and sawn lumber trade and the city's busy port. Even with the dense green forests surrounding it, Tacoma was every bit as lawless and rowdy as Tombstone, Arizona. Like Tombstone and its ilk, early Tacoma was a town dominated by adventurous young men far from home, working hard and playing hard. Bars were plentiful, families scarce, and normal social restraints on outrageous behavior weak or nonexistent.

This colorful environment was populated by equally colorful characters, some of whom apparently became memorable ghosts.

Harry Morgan's ghost takes the form of an overweight, red-faced Irishman. He is dressed in flamboyant poor taste, with a bright green silk vest, shamrock-patterned tie, and loudly checked Irish tweed suit. Morgan was the political boss of early Tacoma. All politicians and cops held their jobs on his approval. Harry, in life, owned a notorious establishment known as Morgan's Gambling House and Comique Theater, a kind of one-stop shopping place for illicit amusement. The bar, it was said, had no locks on the doors, because it was never closed. Gambling was open, though technically illegal, but Morgan was immune from police harassment. He owned the cops. The showgirls who performed risqué dances in the theater were available for more private performances in upstairs rooms.

In short, Morgan's establishment was a well-oiled machine for separating unwary men from their money. They were lucky if money was all they lost. An underground tunnel connected Morgan's bar with the waterfront, a few blocks away. This tunnel was handy for shanghaiing sailors who would wake up with a blinding headache aboard a ship at sea and not see Tacoma again soon, if ever. It is claimed that the spirits of these hapless drunks still stumble through the tunnel late at night, even though the connections between basements were blocked long ago. These unfortunate ghosts just walk right through the now-solid walls segmenting the old tunnel, marching miserably to their fate.

If and when you should glimpse the shade of Harry Morgan near the waterfront on foggy nights, notice the expression on his face. It is said that if he is smiling, political corruption is rampant. If he is frowning, honest citizens can relax—the reformers are in charge.

Then there is the occasional appearance of one of Tacoma's most entertaining spirits, the phantom of the Swearing Deacon. This unique ghost is that of early Tacoma's self-appointed overseer of church attendance at St. Peter's Church, built in 1873. The deacon liked to see the pews filled each Sunday, so every Saturday night, he would tour all the bars. He'd burst into each establishment with an aggressive shout: "Listen to me you drunken [bleep bleep bleep], I want to see you in church tomorrow and you will put fifty cents in the collection plate!" Few argued with the muscular deacon. If his combative spirit shows up at the door of your favorite bar late on Saturday nights, you'd better plan to attend church in the morning. You wouldn't want to cross the spirit of the Swearing Deacon.

Olympic Peninsula and San Juan Islands

THIS REGION RUNS FROM THE STRAIT OF JUAN DE FUCA TO THE COLUM-
bia River and includes the Olympic Mountains with their mid-
latitude rainforests, together with the Pacific Coast and its
picturesque beach towns. Important towns include Port Angeles,
Port Townsend, Longview, and Vancouver.

In this heavily forested region, you can look forward to meeting
the spirit of a friendly old man and a good witch, along with those
of early explorers and a president of the United States. A haunted
lighthouse and ghost canoes add a regional flavor, along with the
ghostly victims of shipwrecks. Bigfoot makes an appearance, as
does an undoubtedly real murderer known as the Human Gorilla.
You will be introduced to the phantom of Sir Frances Drake's fabled
Golden Hind, and the tragic mystery of kidnapped Indian children
will sadden you.

Spirits of the Explorers

The scene is in the Lewis and Clark National Historic Park near
Ilwaco. The two men stand shoulder to shoulder. They are wearing
a tattered and travel-stained mixture of buckskin and worn woolen
garments. They each carry rifles, having learned that danger is seldom far away. The most interesting thing about them is their facial

expressions. Their tanned, ruggedly handsome faces look westward, out to the Pacific Ocean, reflecting a mixture of awe and triumph. They are at the end of a nearly two-and-a-half-year journey to reach this goal, four thousand miles across previously uncharted wilderness. The two phantoms share a few minutes of glory as they witness the sun sinking in the western horizon over the mighty ocean. They are reliving that day in November 1805 when they completed one of the greatest journeys into the unknown ever attempted in North America. Meet the ghosts of Meriwether Lewis and William Clark, extraordinary explorers.

These fascinating spirits are said to appear occasionally at a great number of places, most of them along the trail they blazed from St. Louis, their official starting point, to the mouth of the Columbia River. They had followed the Missouri River west-northwest to its headwaters, crossed the Lemhi Pass across the Rockies, and then followed the Snake and Columbia Rivers to the Pacific, the "western ocean," as they called it. They had encountered blizzards, searing heat, massive storms, and many Indian tribes, friendly and otherwise. Their orders from President Thomas Jefferson included making accurate maps of the largely unknown lands they crossed and observing, recording, and collecting rocks, plant and animal specimens, and native cultural artifacts.

The explorers also would make a strong political statement. Having just purchased the vast Louisiana Territory from France, Jefferson the politician understood the need to strengthen the U.S. claim by exploration. Jefferson the scientist wanted accurate information about the new lands. He also wanted America to advance to the Pacific Northwest, then claimed by Britain, whose merchants and soldiers were crossing Canada. Also, Jefferson had learned about French plans to mount an expedition to what are now Washington, Oregon, Idaho, and Montana. The necessity of an American expedition to the Pacific Coast was apparent, and Jefferson knew just the right man—his friend and fellow Virginian, Meriwether Lewis.

Lewis already was a familiar face at Jefferson's home, Monticello, where he lived for weeks at a time. The president persuaded Congress to allocate $2,500 to Lewis for supplies for this bold adventure. Lewis asked his former army superior, William Clark, to join him as co-leader. Periodically, Lewis and Clark would send a few men back east with collections of dried plants, animal skins and bones, minerals, and Indian materials acquired in traditional exchanges of gifts with local tribes. Once, to the delight of Jefferson's grandchildren, Lewis and Clark sent Jefferson a live prairie dog. Mementos of the expedition are still exhibited where Jefferson put them on display in Monticello's entrance hall.

Lewis was as interesting a man as he is a ghost. Genealogists claim that he is related distantly to both George Washington and Queen Elizabeth II. His diligence and courage as an explorer was rewarded with Lewis being made governor of the Louisiana Territory and gifted with 1,600 acres of land. He died on October 11, 1809, at the age of 35, either by suicide or as the victim of a robbery attempt at a tavern in Tennessee. His family never accepted the suicide story, and his official state monument calls him a murder victim. Clark lived until September 1, 1838. He served as Brigadier General of the Louisiana Territory and an Indian agent.

If you should be lucky enough to catch a brief glimpse of their ghosts, salute them. They were both outstanding patriots who helped make Washington and Oregon part of the United States.

The Chief's Prophecy

Until that night, his retirement to picturesque Port Townsend had been blissfully uneventful, a welcome change from his long career as a professor of mathematics at the University of Washington in Seattle. Recently widowed and tired of big-city life, he found the quiet existence in this charming Victorian-era town much to his liking. His good friend and neighbor who taught history at the university also retired here. They visited one another for drinks and conversation. Life was good and, until that night, uneventful.

He couldn't sleep, even after his customary two double scotches on the rocks. He sat in his darkened living room, gazing out at his moonlit garden when he saw them—well, he was pretty sure he saw them. Or was he just dreaming? First there were four, joined shortly by six more, all in the full ceremonial regalia of Native Americans as they appeared to the first white settlers. As he watched with a mixture of curiosity and disbelief, the little group formed a circle and appeared to be praying. Mesmerized by the sight, he found himself opening the patio door and stepping outside. The ten figures turned slowly in his direction. To his amazement, they slowly morphed from solid form to vapor. Then they evaporated like a morning fog as the sun rose. What was going on?

The next night, he decided to forego alcohol, as he wanted to be cold sober in case his phantom visitors returned. They did. Boldly, or perhaps foolishly, he again ventured out to see them more clearly. This time, they stood their ground, staring directly into his eyes. Without using words or gestures, they somehow communicated to him that they intended no harm, but were visiting the graves of their ancestors. He backed away without comment, locked himself in, and fell into a deep dreamless sleep—unless the whole episode had been a dream.

Fearful of ridicule, he decided to keep quiet about his experience, but eventually he decided to trust his historian friend with the tale. Incredibly, his friend was calmly interested and reassuring. He said he had many such experiences himself. "Chief Seattle himself predicted this," the historian said. "Maybe it was a friendly warning, or maybe it was a veiled threat."

The historian took down an old book and began to read key passages from Chief Seattle's oration to the whites before he signed a treaty with them. He spoke thus:

> To us, the ashes of our ancestors are sacred and their resting place is hallowed ground. You wander far from the graves of your ancestors and seemingly without regret. Your dead cease to love you and the land of their nativity as soon as they pass the portals of the tomb. . . . Our dead never forget the beautiful world that gave them being. And when the last red man shall have perished and the memory of my tribe shall have become a myth among the white men, these shores will swarm with the invisible dead of my tribe, and when your children's children think themselves alone in the field, the store, the shop, upon the highway or in the silence of the pathless woods, they will not be alone. . . . At night when the streets of your cities and villages are silent and you think deserted, they will throng with the returning hosts that once filled and still love this beautiful land. The white man will never be alone. Let him be just and deal kindly with my people, for the dead are not powerless. Dead, did I say? There is no death, only a change of worlds.

The book closed, the two friends sat together as dusk fell. Perhaps tonight they would see more of the phantom Native Americans.

Phantoms of Fort Vancouver

Among the many ghosts said to hang around old Fort Vancouver are two very different spirits: John McLoughlin and Ulysses S. Grant. Vancouver, once the head of oceangoing navigation on the Columbia River, is Washington's oldest town. Fort Vancouver is the oldest functioning military base in the Pacific Northwest; its beginnings go back to the old Hudson's Bay Trading Company post when England and the United States both claimed the old Oregon Territory and encouraged their citizens to homestead there.

A treaty signed in 1818 gave both countries equal rights in the area, an essentially unworkable compromise. The two nations were like a pair of wrestlers circling each other warily, watching for an unguarded moment to pounce. Hudson's Bay, a private company that often operated as an arm of the English crown, appointed Dr. John McLoughlin as the chief of its trading post at Vancouver. McLoughlin was an impressive figure. Tall, white-headed, and dressed entirely in black, he was known as an aggressive and ambitious administrator. He was tough on the Native Americans, who called him the "White Headed Eagle," always favoring the whites in any dispute.

McLoughlin's trading post was also a fort, and he extended aid and protection equally to both English and American settlers, which got him into trouble with his bosses back home. He was fired from his post for being "too friendly with Americans." He invested in land near Oregon City when the 1846 treaty established the current boundary with Canada. Poor, unlucky McLoughlin was thrown off his land claim, because he was not then an American citizen. He died in obscurity, an impoverished, bitter old man, scorned and denied rights by both the English and Americans. His unhappy ghost is said to wander aimlessly around the old fort area, with a profoundly disappointed look on his face.

The other major historical phantom is believed to be the spirit of Ulysses S. Grant, Civil War hero and President of the United States.

In 1852–53, Grant was stationed at Fort Vancouver, a frustrating and boring time for the future general. Vancouver then was a long way from any action, military or otherwise. Grant's supernatural presence is more frequently smelled than seen. His cigar-smoking habit is said to produce a strong scent in the Grant House on Officers' Row. The house, the oldest on the row, was never lived in by Grant, but he did spend a lot of his spare time there, because it was the officers' club in his day. Grant was not a drunk; he could "hold his liquor" as they said. Evidently, he held a lot of liquor. He was known as a "four-finger" drinker. Each shot of whiskey filled a tumbler to the depth of a finger's width, so a four-finger drinker was drinking from a glass filled a hand's breadth full. Grant smoked at least six cigars a day; eventually he died of throat cancer. The odor of his cigars can still be detected in the Grant House, now occupied by a prestigious restaurant.

Less famous ghosts are alleged to appear on occasion in the vicinity of old Fort Vancouver. One is a sentry in nineteenth-century uniform who paces along Officers' Row at night. Another spirit is that of a Native American woman, believed to be the ghost of a person whose bones were found under the auditorium building at the post. She was wearing "trade beads," glass beads often used in trading with Native Americans in the mid-nineteenth century. Her ghost still has the trade bead necklace around her neck.

The Lighthouse Phantoms

It is common on America's Atlantic coast to hear tales of haunted lighthouses. The Pacific coast is no different. Lighthouses are likely to be old, isolated, and intimately connected with tragic deaths, all characteristics associated with hauntings.

Cape Disappointment State Park, near Ilwaco, contains not just one, but two haunted lighthouses, Cape Disappointment Light and nearby North Head Light. Both are said to be haunted by the phantoms of shipwreck victims and former lighthouse keepers.

Many people share the sour suspicion that in order for local authorities to install a traffic light at an intersection, a fatal accident or two must happen there first. It seems to be so with lighthouses as well. The oldest lighthouse on the West Coast, Cape Disappointment Light was commissioned in 1856. It is still a functioning light.

Built of brick, it is only 53 feet tall, but its light is 220 feet above the waves, as it is built on a promontory. Although at least 230 ships have come to grief on the submerged bars at the mouth of the Columbia River, one shipwreck in particular seems to have inspired building a light at the cape. In a terrific storm in 1853, the schooner *Vandalla* wrecked, killing everyone aboard. Two rocky indentations along this section of coast are named for this disaster—Dead Man's Hollow and Beard's Hollow, named after the *Vandalla*'s captain, Edward Beard, whose body washed ashore there. The *Vandalla* was found floating bottom side-up. Those who attempted to salvage the ship claim to have heard loud hammering sounds from within the hull. When they cut through the hull, they found only bodies, dead for many hours. The would-be rescuers are said to have had horrific nightmares of corpses frantically pounding in the sturdy oak walls of their upside-down ship, gasping for fresh air. The ghosts of the *Vandalla*'s crew supposedly terrorized the neighborhood of their disaster until Cape Disappointment got its light.

Unfortunately, the dead did not rest for long. Because of the configuration of the coast there, the new light could not be seen by the ships approaching it from the north, at least not until it was too late. Another lighthouse was necessary. Despite the grim advocacy of the many ghosts, the North Head Light wasn't built until 1898. The ghosts of many shipwreck victims are so angry about this long delay that it is claimed that they still haunt both lighthouses. These phantoms are described as being clad in soaking wet, seaweed-draped clothing. Their eye sockets are empty, as crabs feast on the eyes of the dead first.

An especially interesting ghost is that of an early lighthouse keeper for the Cape Disappointment Light, Joel Munson. Joel was a very conscientious man who took his responsibilities most seriously. Every day he would carry gallons of oil up the steps to fuel the light that night. He would clean and polish the complex Fresnel lens, designed to focus the light so it could be seen for miles. He would stay up all night to ensure the spring-driven mechanism that revolved the light continued to function. Munson was so distressed by so frequently having to fish corpses out of the sea that he organized a life-saving service to try to rescue the victims of shipwrecks.

According to local legend, Munson's ghost would show up again to tend the light if one of his successors fell ill or had an accident that prevented them from tending to their duties. When the living light keeper or his substitute finally showed up, they would find the light freshly refueled and cleaned. Even now, when the light's operation is fully automated, the shadow of a man can be seen atop the light, checking that all is well with the functions of the vital light. Is Joel Munson still on duty? Some think so.

The Ghostly Green Light

The house is a real charmer—a beautifully preserved Queen Anne-style structure in a neighborhood of similarly ornate Victorian homes in Port Townsend. The town boasts a large collection of such buildings, as it actually is a kind of fossilized town. After a major financial collapse in 1890, its population abruptly declined, leaving enough people to maintain the houses, but no incentive to tear them down to be replaced with more up-to-date designs.

These exuberantly built Victorians are replete with towers, turrets, bays, and wraparound porches, all trimmed with wooden gingerbread details. They each have a history, but one in particular is known to be haunted. The haunted house sits atop a low, flat bluff just behind the waterfront. It has a commanding view of Admiralty Inlet, and of course, ships likewise have a fine view of the house, which brings us to the ghost story.

Port Townsend in the 1870s and 1880s was a busy, cosmopolitan place, as its customs house made it an official port of entry. Foreign vessels filled the bay and commerce flourished, most of it legal. A number of local lads, however, had discovered that smuggling could be very profitable indeed. Proximity to Canada offered many opportunities to make a fortune overnight, bringing in untaxed goods and illegal immigrants, mostly Chinese, from Vancouver and Victoria. The only flaw in these get-rich-quick schemes was the possibility of getting caught by the Coast Guard. Smugglers caught in the act had their boats confiscated and they went to prison for a long time.

The lure of quick money proved irresistible for many local fishermen. Bringing back a few boatloads of luxury goods, good whiskey, or illegal Chinese immigrants instead of salmon, tuna, red snapper, or cod could set a man up for life.

A poor young fisherman fell in love with the lovely daughter of a prosperous banker, who lived in a splendid new house on the bluff. The girl was very much in love, but her parents did not approve. "Our Rose is used to the finer things in life," they admonished their daughter's suitor. "She wouldn't be happy in a fisherman's shack."

Rose and her lover conspired to transform him into a prosperous business owner, one who owned his own ship's supply house. All it would take would be a few successful smuggling runs, which would have to be timed to avoid Coast Guard patrols. Conveniently, Rose's older sister was married to a captain in the Coast Guard, a man of great courage and integrity who invariably commanded the cutter charged with policing Port Townsend Bay. If the captain was home, his cutter was tied up at its wharf, and the coast was clear for smuggling.

When Rose learned of the captain's presence at home, or in her parents' home, she would signal her intended by displaying a light in the window of the turret in the corner of her house. An oil lamp with a green glass shade would signal a safe time to enter the bay with an illegal cargo. No light, no go. The scheme worked perfectly, once, then twice. "One more trip!" promised the fisherman, "and I'll have enough money to buy the store and marry you."

That last trip was planned for Rose's birthday, when her brother-in-law would surely come to her party unless his duty called. He showed up in civilian clothing, meaning he was not on call that evening and his ship was not on duty. Rose lit the green lamp, rejoicing in the knowledge that this was the last time her lover would be a smuggler.

At the close of the party, the captain proudly announced that he had been promoted to a desk job, no more night patrols for him. "Yes sir," he bragged, "the cutter is now in the hands of my lieutenant!"

"Is it out on patrol now?" asked a panicky Rose. "Yes indeed," was the answer. Too late did she extinguish the green light. Her lover was caught, convicted, and imprisoned. Rose lost her mind and convinced herself that it never happened. For the rest of her life she maintained the green light in the turret room. Her ghost continues to keep that forlornly hopeful light lit to this day.

Ghost Canoes

The canoes are an impressive sight. Each one was painstakingly carved from a single cedar log. Master canoe builders selected a cedar as flawless as possible, one with few major branches on its straight lower trunk. They used obsidian axes to fell the tree and strip off bark and branches. Hot stones were used to char the interior to make it easier to shape and to retard splitting. The finished dugout canoes were waterproofed by rubbing in many coats of oil from the livers of dogfish, a small shark. Natural pigments were added to the fish oil to make red, green, black, and white paints. The canoes are beautiful and were of great importance to the Wahkiakum and Cathlamet Indians of the lower Columbia River country. They were used in fishing and whaling, trading, and war. They also were used as coffins to carry their deceased owners on their last voyages.

It is in their coffin role that the ghost canoes of the Columbia are seen. Tradition holds that they float out to sea only on floods combined with high tides, so they are rarely seen now. Floods on the Columbia just don't happen on the scale of the old days. The river has been tamed and regulated by the great dams built upstream from Cathlamet. The occasional high-water periods, when combined with a spring tide, can still send the ghost canoes sailing majestically out to sea, however, carrying the dead to the "flood of life" as prophesized in local Indian lore.

The tribes of the lower Columbia had a special honor for deceased chiefs, shamans, and other important people. The corpse was dressed in fine fur robes and beads and trinkets. They were laid out in their canoe, which was then placed high in cottonwood trees along the river banks. The prow of the canoe was pointing west toward the ocean. When the next great flood occurred, the canoe would be floated free of its perch in the tree. As the canoe surges westward with the receding tide, legend holds that the canoe's occupant would sit up and face the west. For this reason, the deceased always was positioned on his back, feet toward the prow, so that as he sat up again, he would face the setting sun. The spirits of the dead flew to the sun as it sank into the great ocean, thus entering the world of the spirits.

It is believed that the last actual coffin canoe was hoisted into the riverbank trees around 1850, but the ghosts of the canoes still sail downriver on receding spring tides. Shimmering with an eerie greenish glow, they carry their dead passengers out to sea. Their dead occupants sit up as the canoe approaches the open sea, looking forward to joining the spirits of their ancestors, endlessly repeating their final journey on earth. The best place to experience this ghostly sight is said to be at Coffin Rock, a small promontory about six miles east of Cathlamet on scenic Route 4.

The Phantom of the Golden Hind

It happens during winter storms off the state's Pacific coastline. Not everyone who sees this apparition is brave enough, or perhaps foolhardy enough, to tell others of their experience. Who would believe them? The likelihood of being scorned or mocked as a drunk or someone pathetically eager for attention is enough to discourage most sailors.

Those brave enough to tell the story describe a three-masted, wooden sailing ship of antique design. Her wind-filled sails are moving her quickly before the storm. Her proud flag shows a red cross of St. George, England's patron saint, on a white field. Curiously, the swift ship leaves no wake as she seems to fly past the observer. Then, suddenly, the ship disappears as though it was never there. Some claim to have read *Golden Hind* across the high, narrow stern of the phantom ship just before she vanished from sight.

There really was a *Golden Hind* in these waters in 1579, and she was captained by none other than the famous Sir Francis Drake. Or is that the infamous Sir Francis Drake? It depends on your viewpoint. To the Spanish, he was a ruthless pirate, one who had diabolical powers as a navigator. To the English, he was a national hero, the savior of their nation.

Actually, Drake's own countrymen agreed with the Spanish that he possessed supernatural powers. Drake, it was widely believed, had traded his soul to the Devil in exchange for great prowess at sea. Drake, it was whispered, could not only navigate safely through tremendous storms, but he could cast spells that raised storms that destroyed his enemies. He was said to be a wizard—a magician

with supernatural powers. He had a magic mirror that showed him the position of ships anywhere in the world.

After demonstrating his uncanny luck in finding and capturing Spanish treasure ships in the Caribbean, Drake was asked by Queen Elizabeth to sail into the Pacific Ocean and pursue more Spanish gold. He did so, capturing about $10 million in gold from one ship alone off the west coast of Panama. With the *Golden Hind* riding low in the water from all that gold, and Spanish warships on his trail, Drake sailed north along North America's coast. He sailed as far as Canada's Vancouver Island and may have reached the Alaskan panhandle area before sailing west to Asia. He may have landed on the coast of California or Washington in order to repair his ship, but this cannot be proven. Drake's ship's log and records were classified "top secret" by the queen and later lost in a fire. The phantom of the *Golden Hind* may be seen off Washington's coast, however, fulfilling Drake's pledge to sail his route around the world again many times as a ghost to celebrate his great achievement. He was only the second navigator to sail around the world (Spain's Ferdinand Magellan was first).

Sailing his phantom *Golden Hind* off Washington's coast is only one of Drake's supernatural exploits. He fell in love with a noblewoman named Elizabeth Sudenham. Her family would not allow her to marry a commoner, and so Drake went to sea with a promise to come back a rich man. After waiting a year (it took Drake more than two years to sail around the world) Elizabeth was about to marry another. Drake allegedly fired a magical cannonball halfway around the world to land at her feet as she was about to marry. She canceled the wedding. The "cannonball" later turned out to be an iron meteorite and is in a museum. Could Drake command the very heavens? His future wife thought so.

If you should spot the phantom *Golden Hind* off Washington's coast, it would be prudent to "dip" your flag (lower and raise it again quickly) as a sign of respect. You wouldn't want an iron meteorite to come your way. Incidentally, the Latin version of Drake is *draco*, which means "dragon," a mythical beast of great cunning and enormous power. Perhaps Francis Drake really was in league with the Devil.

The Eternal Embrace

When their bodies were retrieved from the sea off the mouth of the Columbia River, they were locked in an embrace. The two corpses held each other tightly and seemed to be staring into one another's sightless eyes. Their sodden clothing was new and stylish. Brand new matching gold bands adorned their hands. To no one's surprise, the pair turned out to be newlyweds, traveling on their honeymoon aboard the ill-fated *General Warren*.

The *General Warren* was one of a long list of ships lost off the stormy coast of the Evergreen State. Forty other souls perished in addition to the entwined lovers when it sank on January 28, 1852.

The infamous Bermuda Triangle is no more fearsome than Washington's coastline, where at least two thousand shipwrecks have occurred over the centuries, causing more than seven hundred deaths by drowning and exposure. The mouth of the Columbia River is an especially treacherous area for ships. The "great river of the north," as it was called, focuses its surging current "like a gigantic fire hose," in the words of some sailors. All the water drained from an area the size of France suddenly meets the powerful Japan Current, which sweeps across the north Pacific to meet the Columbia's discharge almost head on. As these currents collide, the Columbia's current slows, depositing a shallow bar of debris across its mouth. The two natural channels through the bar forced sailing ships at one point to turn sideways to the prevailing winds and currents, a sure way to disaster.

The wreck of the *General Warren* may have contributed to the federal government's decision to build a lighthouse on Cape Disappointment in 1856 and on neighboring North Head in 1898. Were these much-needed lighthouses inspired by the area's notorious reputation as a "graveyard of the Pacific," a graveyard populated by hundreds of ghosts?

It is widely believed that ghosts are associated with untimely deaths and there have been many such along this coast. Allegedly, the ghosts of three famous shipwrecks haunt the vicinity of Cape Disappointment. Along with the forty-two victims of the *General Warren* are the victims of the forty-two lost of the *Queen of the*

Pacific (1883) and the thirty-four victims of the wrecked *Iowa* in 1936.

Most of the cape's phantoms are pathetic and harmless, never interacting with the living like the tragic honeymooners still in their eternal embrace. Some spirits, however, are visibly angry and not resigned to their fate. These disturbing ghosts might be the products of treacherous greed rather than nature's storms and currents.

No fewer than twenty-five old sailing vessels sank off the Washington coast between 1890 and 1910. All were relics of the wooden sailing ship era—barely seaworthy in their old age and no longer profitable in the days of iron and steam. Were they deliberately sent out in stormy weather along an admittedly dangerous coast so that their owners could collect the insurance? That was the unproven suspicion at the time and that may be the testimony of the angry ghosts.

If you ever encounter the ghosts of Cape Disappointment, pray that you meet the tragic honeymooners in their eternal embrace. They represent undying love, while the ghosts of the supposed insurance wrecks surely represent vengeance.

The Phantoms of Mystery Bay

Among the mysteries of Mystery Bay is how and when it got its name. The most widespread explanation goes back to the 1920s, during Prohibition. Prohibition was based on the evidently erroneous assumption that when the manufacture and distribution of alcoholic beverages was outlawed, Americans would stop consuming alcohol. No one disputes that this did not follow. Instead, the illegal manufacture and importation of alcoholic beverages flourished. Otherwise law-abiding citizens routinely broke the law, which finally was overturned in 1933.

Illegal stills, operated with little skill in unsanitary conditions, produced a wretched-tasting, occasionally lethal product, one that could not compete with distilleries functioning legally outside the United States. Smuggling alcoholic beverages from Canada down to the thirsty residents of the Evergreen State became an almost honored profession. With Canada so close as a supply source, and with so many potential customers living on or close to Puget Sound, anyone with a small boat, a sense of adventure, and a conviction that Prohibition was a silly and ultimately unenforceable law could make a fast fortune.

Speed, stealth, and creative thinking were the tactics employed by the smugglers. Mystery Bay supposedly got its name from the frustrated Coast Guard, whose cutters often chased smugglers into that bay only to have their quarry disappear. Where could they have gone? That was the mystery of Mystery Bay, which is really just a protected cove of Skow Bay on the western side of Marrowstone Island, just off Admiralty Inlet.

Some smugglers relied on pure speed, outrunning pursuing Coast Guard boats by the brute power of their engines. It was the stealth practitioners who helped give Mystery Bay its name, and it is the alleged phantoms of the sneakier smugglers who perpetuate the mysteries of the bay right up to the present.

Achieving superior speed was less taxing on the intellectual powers of would-be smugglers. In fact, it was downright easy. At the end of World War I, cheap surplus aircraft engines were readily available. Local boat builders would put one, sometimes two, aircraft engines into a narrow, shallow-draft hull, creating a sort of rocket with a keel. Called "cigarette boats," because of their slender shapes, these craft could easily outrun anything the Coast Guard was using; however, they consumed high quantities of fuel, could not carry much of a payload, and were notoriously unstable in high-speed turns.

It was two slower but craftily operated boats that produced the mystery in Mystery Bay. According to some, they, or rather their phantoms, still cruise these waters on foggy, moonless nights. The *President Coolidge* was captained by a man known as the Magician. He is said to have made regular trips to Victoria, British Columbia, to "whet his whistle" at the bar of the famous Empress Hotel on that city's waterfront, but stoutly denied smuggling. He sailed quite openly, in full daylight, and made no attempt to evade the Coast Guard. He would cheerfully submit to searches of his schooner; contraband liquor was never found. Everyone knew he was smuggling, but how? On his deathbed, the Magician revealed his secret. Crates of liquor, balanced just so by cork floats, were placed in string nets fastened to the hull underwater. When the *President*

Coolidge was underway, the net would surge up into the wake, just under the surface. While stopped, the net would dangle straight down from the hull, almost impossible to detect. To this day, the ghost of the *President Coolidge* still cruises into Mystery Bay, only to disappear if another boat approaches.

The other phantom ship of Mystery Bay is the ghost of the *Sable*, which is Latin for black. The *Sable*'s hull was painted dead black. Her sails were black. She carried no running lights on her smuggling excursions, which of course were on moonless nights, preferably in fog. She was the naval equivalent of a stealth bomber—almost invisible. It is said that the *Sable* still sneaks in and out of Mystery Bay, glimpsed only briefly from other boats in the vicinity.

If you should happen to spot the *Sable* or the *Coolidge* on their ghostly voyages, you might salute them with a drink. Of Canadian whiskey, please.

Manresa Castle's Ghosts

Port Townsend, on the northeast tip of the Olympic Peninsula, is a charming historic town with an interesting collection of Victorian architecture. The town's maritime history and its supernatural history are linked by one of its more famous ghosts.

Founded in 1851, Port Townsend was the location of the only customs house on Puget Sound. This meant that any and all ships from foreign ports had to first report there to process their paperwork. Foreign consulates, banks, hotels, and merchant's exchanges prospered there, and local millionaires built some very impressive residences. One of the more spectacular mansions was Manresa Castle, built in 1892 to look like a castle on Germany's Rhine River. When a long-anticipated transcontinental railroad terminus failed to be built, Port Townsend entered an economic decline, and the huge castle became a thirty-nine-room hotel. Shortly after its conversion to a hotel, tragedy struck. The suicide of a young woman produced Manresa Castle's most famous, though not sole, ghost.

The lovely young lady, whose name is lost to history, was at Manresa preparing for her wedding. The reception was to be held in the castle's romantic dining room, with its high ceilings and elaborate fireplaces. Her joyful anticipation was turned to heart-wrenching sorrow by a terse telegram. Her future husband, a sailor, had been lost at sea. A freak wave had washed him overboard during a storm. Devastated by the news, the woman returned to her third-floor room (number 306, if you are a ghost hunter). There, she allegedly donned her wedding dress, applied makeup, put her hair up in an elaborate style, and jumped out the window to her death.

There is an unsubstantiated rumor that the tragic young woman can be heard singing in the bathroom of her former room. She is supposedly singing romantic ballads of her day; each supernatural concert is said to end with her humming Mendelssohn's "Wedding March." Then there is silence, followed by the sound of a window being raised, ending in a scream.

In another version of this story, the woman in her wedding gown is seen dancing very late in the empty dining room. She appears to be waltzing in the arms of a handsome man wearing a dripping-wet sailor suit. His tangled hair is festooned with seaweed.

Another of Manresa's ghosts is that of a monk, wearing a dark brown, hooded robe cinched by a white rope. He is wearing simple sandals. No one knows who he is, or was, or what he is doing there.

Beautifully restored, elegant Manresa Castle is now a popular bed-and-breakfast. Enjoy your stay. It is a charming place in a charming town, with or without supernatural guests appearing. The alleged ghosts never interact with the living, merely providing other guests with an interesting story.

Seeing is Believing

Seeing is believing, or so they say. Not that you can always believe in what you think you see. One family in Longview has come to think that believing is seeing—that if your mind wants to believe that a familiar sight is there, then your eyes will obediently see it. Or, maybe your eyes receive an image sensed by the spiritual or paranormal parts of your brain.

For years, the whole family had waved cheerfully to a stranger. Well, he wasn't truly a stranger, because they knew where he lived, but they did not know his name or personal history. The children had initiated their friendly if distant relationship when they were quite young. The route home from shopping led them right past the man several times a week. The man was old, but the house was much older. It was one of those structures that had led several lives, judging by its appearance. Built in the 1890s as a suburban home for a large and prosperous family, it was converted into a gas station in the 1920s. Then, in the late 1960s, the woefully old-fashioned gas station, unable to compete with the new chains, was fittingly converted into an antique shop. "More like an overly ambitious junk store" was the common assessment.

So there it sat, on its corner, a weathered old building where customers were few and interest waning. An old man sat on the deep side porch, morning and afternoon, sunshine or rain, winter or summer. In summer, he wore an old-fashioned straw hat; in winter, he donned a warm cap with earflaps. He seemed to be a permanent fixture, like a piece of furniture. The family even wondered if the familiar figure might be an advertising mannequin. Until he waved, that is.

One day, as their car slowed for the tight turn, the kids impulsively waved at him. To their delight, the old man gave them a warm, broad smile and a return wave. Ever after the exchange of greetings was part of any trip in the car. He seemed to be always there, always alert to their waves, and always warmly responsive.

The years went by, the children grew up, but the cheerful exchange of silent greetings continued. Then the day came when the mother of the family decided to stop at the antique store in search of old costume jewelry with which she made Christmas tree ornaments. She thought she saw the old man on the porch as she drove up the driveway, but he was not there when she got out of the car. Having made her purchase, she inquired about the old man.

"Old man?" was the first puzzled response, followed quickly by, "Oh, you must mean Uncle Charley. He used to live with us but he's been dead for four years now. He used to love sitting in that porch, watching the world go by. And he loved to wave at folks."

"But we've waved to him for twenty years, including just this week," said the disbelieving customer. She consulted a psychic, who explained what must have happened. "The old man's spiritual energy must have imprinted itself on his customary rocking chair out on that porch. He so enjoyed his living moments in that place that his spirit returned to its zone of comfort and love. You and your family were so used to seeing him there that your minds picked up the spiritual essence he left behind and converted it to a familiar, friendly image."

So, if seeing isn't always believing, believers can see. Keep waving. There are worse things than communing with a friendly spirit, aren't there?

The Good Witch

To be sure, there are few witch stories in the Evergreen State, especially compared with New England. Interestingly, the witch story that was told by old-timers in Port Townsend has a New England connection.

Do you believe in witches, or more accurately, do you believe in witchcraft? Before you deny any such belief, consider this. If you believe in luck, luck of any kind, you believe that unseen forces or influences, good or bad, can shape our lives. That surely at least puts you in the same zip code as believers in witchcraft. People who wear lucky ties or jewelry or play lucky numbers in the lottery have something in common with believers in witchcraft.

Just how real are witches? It might depend on your belief system. An old saying in New England goes, "Where folks believe in witches, witches are; but where they don't believe, there ain't no witches thar."

So, are there, or were there, witches thar? A hundred and fifty years ago, the community consensus in Port Townsend was that Aunt Fanny was a witch, and a good one at that. Aunt Fanny was not anybody's aunt, but she was everybody's aunt—an honorific title earned by her many kindnesses to children, especially poor children. Aunt Fanny had been brought to Port Townsend as a toddler in the 1850s. Her father, a Maine sea captain, had decided that the West Coast opportunities were superior to those back east. Fanny's mother knew a thing or two about witchcraft and found an apt pupil in her young daughter. Fanny is said to have decided to use her knowledge of supernatural powers for good, not evil.

Aunt Fanny made herself popular in her community by distributing food to the needy. Families fallen on hard times would be given a basket of fresh eggs, a whole ham, or even a freshly killed turkey. Poor children could count on a large birthday cake on their special day. She seemed to have a limitless supply of home-baked molasses cookies to give to any and all children she met on her rounds.

Aunt Fanny had inherited a nice house from her parents, but had no known source of income. How could she afford to be so generous? Curiosity overcame respect and caution for two neighborhood youngster, who decided to spy on Aunt Fanny. They stealthily approached her house one evening to peer in the windows. What they saw was truly amazing. Fanny took a large, colorful scarf, which she customarily wore around her neck, and hung it over a large bowl. She then twisted the fabric and wrung from it fresh milk, muttering incantations in an unknown tongue. Next, she placed the scarf over a large empty plate, said a few words, and uncovered a dozen eggs. An empty roasting pan was made to produce a roast turkey, followed by a whole baked salmon. As the boys watched fascinated, she filled her kitchen with supernaturally produced food that looked and smelled real and delicious.

At one point, Aunt Fanny looked over at the window. She smiled and just went back to her magic. The boys later crept quietly away. It wasn't until they got home that they each discovered a large, warm molasses cookie in their shirt pockets. From then on, the word gradually spread that Aunt Fanny was a witch, but she was a very good, kind, and generous witch—a kind of community angel. An unspoken pact evolved: Treat Aunt Fanny with respect and keep silent about her awesome powers. Every community could use a good witch.

An Encounter with Bigfoot

One thing the campers could agree upon was its size. Whatever it was, it was big. Eight feet was the most common estimate of the creature's height. Of course, this guess was made in the moment of panic when the creature charged, snarling and grunting as it ran directly at the terrified group. Fortunately for the campers, whatever it was veered off at the last minute, tearing away at an angle that took it into the dense forest into which it soon disappeared. As suddenly as it had happened, it was gone.

For the four campers, it was a truly unforgettable experience, but also one which all were reluctant to mention to others. Among

themselves, they decided that it must have been a Bigfoot. But who could they tell who wouldn't doubt them, even mock them? Tales of Bigfoot sightings often elicit amused disbelief and questions about the sanity, sobriety, and motives of the reporter.

The disturbing incident occurred in Olympic National Park, almost a million acres of wilderness lying only fifty miles due west of Seattle. At the heart of the Olympic Peninsula, Mount Olympus rises 7,965 feet above sea level. The edges of the national park and national forest surrounding it are easily reached by car, but the key word here is "edges." No road crosses the park, which retains its true wilderness character. In many ways, the Olympics look more like coastal Alaska than the shores of Puget Sound. Fifty-seven glaciers creep down the slopes of the Olympic Mountain range. Huge trees that were already centuries old when the first European explorers arrived still stand. Some western valleys of these mountains regularly receive between twelve and fourteen feet of rain every year. The result is a mid-latitude rainforest like the Amazon without the parrots and monkeys.

In such dense woods, even an eight-foot tall Bigfoot could be out of sight, but only a few feet away. The lush forest of fir, spruce, cedar, and pine supports an abundant array of wildlife—elk, deer, black bears, bobcats, and cougars. There is little doubt that a breeding population of Bigfoot could find enough food—even ferns reach four-foot heights. Staying hidden in the hundreds of thousands of acres of nearly inaccessible forest would be no trick for Bigfoot.

The experience of the four campers in Olympic National Park is typical. The two young couples had hiked in from the end of an unpaved road, setting up their camp in a small meadow. It was almost dusk when they gathered around a campfire. It was then that they heard rustling in nearby trees and undergrowth. A powerful stench overcame them as the wind shifted. Thinking it might be a bear, they threw more wood on the fire and began making as much noise as they could. Then they noticed a pair of eyes reflecting the firelight; the eyes were at least seven feet above the ground.

Suddenly, a huge ape-like figure charged into their little clearing. Covered in coarse, black hair, it was about eight feet tall and ran quickly on two feet, swerving away at the last minute. After the campers' understandable panic subsided, they took turns staying awake until daybreak, when they broke camp and returned to their vehicles. By agreement, they told only their closest, most trustworthy friends about their encounter with Bigfoot. How many would believe them anyway?

That Darn Pig!

That darn pig! It was at it again, rooting in the garden, ripping up plants, and generally making a mess. Almost automatically, the man reached for his rifle, then thought better of it. The last time he'd fired at the marauding hog, he'd gotten a stern warning from an irate cop. Discharging a weapon in town, disturbing the peace, and being a darn fool were mentioned as grounds for spending a night in Friday Harbor's jail the next time. Besides, the pig wasn't real—it was the phantom of a pig that almost started a war between England and the United States, and that was way back in 1859.

It was a very tense time then in the San Juan Islands. The boundary between Canada and the United States had been fixed at the forty-ninth parallel by treaty, with all of Vancouver Island going to the British. But what about all the little islands between the mainland and Vancouver Island? Both parties in the dispute claimed them all. Both the British and American governments encouraged their citizens to settle on the islands. Both sides sent troops to protect the rights of their citizens. Everyone was on edge; it was a war waiting to happen.

And then it almost happened. A pig belonging to an Englishman, Charles Griffin, broke down a fence and raided the garden of an American, Lyman Cutler. It rooted up and ate all of Cutler's potatoes, carrots, and beets. Cutler shot the pig and threw a barbecue for his American neighbors. Griffin wanted money for his pig. Cutler said no way. The pig was trespassing and deserved to be shot and eaten, and furthermore, any British soldiers who might object would be shot too. Both sides sent more troops to defend their own people and their own pigs. For a while it looked likely that the two nations would go to war. Then, someone suggested throwing a party. The Americans would bring food—ham sandwiches!—and the English would bring scotch. Everyone relaxed after the third or fourth drink. International arbitration awarded the islands to America. So ended the Pig War.

But why is the spirit of that pig still roaming about San Juan Island? Is this phantom a relic of all the negative psychic energy that once nearly exploded into war? Maybe the ghostly pig serves as a reminder that some wars, at least, are avoidable by using some common sense. Pass the bacon, and keep that gun's safety catch on.

The Spirit of the Beast Man

Almost a century after his violent death, the fearsome spirit of the Beast Man allegedly still roams the densely forested mountains of the Olympic Peninsula. A quick glimpse of this beast man was enough to freeze the blood of the bravest observer; the sight of his ghost still can induce a lifetime of horrible nightmares.

There are many gruesome and terrifying legends about this Beast Man; the truly scary part is that most of them are absolutely true. For three years, from 1910 to 1913, the Olympic wilderness was terrorized by an all-too real monster known variously as the "Wild Man of the Olympics," the "Beast Man," and the "Human Gorilla." No gorilla ever tracked and killed people the way the beast man did, however, seemingly without cause or mercy.

The real name of this pitiless murderer was John Turnow (or Tornow). He escaped from an institution for the criminally insane in Salem, Oregon, in 1910 and began his legendary rampage in northwestern Washington shortly thereafter. No one really knows how many people were victims of Turnow's three-year orgy of blood. Many a logger, hunter, fisherman, or homesteader disappeared without a trace during Turnow's reign of terror. It is known for certain that he killed two young hunters near Grays Harbor, two lawmen near Satsop, and two more sheriffs in the firefight that finally killed him near Montesano.

At one point, a bounty of $5,000, a fortune at the time, was placed on Turnow's head, dead or alive. As many as a thousand men at a time combed the woods searching for him, but he eluded capture until April 16, 1913, when three deputy sheriffs stumbled on his hideout. Turnow killed two of them before the third shot him.

In life, the Beast Man was an awesome and bone-chilling sight. He stood six feet, five inches tall and weighed 250 pounds, all of it hard muscle. His long black hair was tangled and greasy. He wore clothing he made himself out of animal skins and tree bark. He was an expert hunter of animals and men, patiently tracking his quarry and sometimes driving his victims into pits lined with sharpened sticks and cleverly disguised with vegetation. Several hunters and loggers reported that they had been followed by the Beast Man, who would suddenly and dramatically reveal himself to them, then laugh at their panicked retreat.

Did he stalk men just for fun? Some believed that Turnow had acquired a taste for human livers—this organ was said to be missing from mutilated bodies discovered in his hunting territory.

There is no doubt that John Turnow was a skilled outdoorsman, a loner who knew the woods and could literally live off the land. He was the dark side of an American ideal—self-reliant, crafty, and experienced at mastering nature. He was, according to contemporaries, "like smoke." He moved through the forest unseen and unheard, a master of stealth and cunning.

His ghost, naturally, is a model of animal-like perseverance on the hunt, a trait we could admire if we were not the hunted. Was that a human figure we glimpsed briefly in the early-morning mists of the forest? Were those human eyes staring out at us from the underbrush? Is that uneasy feeling that we are being followed just our imagination? For hundreds of generations, people have had a heightened awareness of possible danger in the deep, dark woods. When we say, "We're not out of the woods yet," we mean we're not out of danger yet. Enjoy your next camping trip in the Olympic wilderness. But stay alert for the shade of the Beast Man. This phantom is said to enjoy stalking the living, though his weapon now is fright rather than a rifle.

The Haunted Place

There are two reasons why the small town of Yacolt is of interest to visitors. The happier reason is that the place serves as the departure point of the Chelatchie Prairie Railroad, a tourist line offering train trips through the surrounding countryside. The second, more foreboding reason is that the very name Yacolt is derived from a Native American word meaning "haunted place." Local tradition holds that a truly horrific incident gave the place its name and that two centuries after this event, the ghosts of the victims and their guardian spirits still haunt the neighborhood.

The disappearance of a child has to rank as any parent's worst nightmare. Many parents briefly have experienced the sheer panic of loss, followed by the enormous surge of relief at an emotional reunion. Even a few moments of separation produce terrible anxieties in parents and children. Every parent can imagine the agony of the slow realization of permanent loss.

Yacolt is situated in a small prairie cupped in the western flanks of the Cascade Range near Bells Mountain, some twenty-five miles north of the Columbia River. These prairies, or open meadows, sometimes are natural but more often are the result of the Native Americans of the past setting fires to create them. The local tribes had observed that tasty huckleberries grew more profusely on lands where recent forest fires had occurred; the fires allowed more sunlight to reach the ground freshly fertilized by wood ashes. Fires were set in late winter when snow still blanketed the land, reducing the chances of fires raging out of control.

The huckleberries were gathered in summer, usually by children while their fathers were catching salmon on their runs upstream to spawn. Five children were out on the prairie with their hand-woven baskets, gently stripping the berries from their low bushes. One minute they were there, the next moment they were gone. Fear raced through the tribe like summer fire. Where could the children be? What could have happened? Had they been kidnapped by a rival tribe to be held for ransom or used as slaves? Such things had happened before, but not this time. No word of ransom demand was heard. The dread suspicion began to grow that the children might have been stolen for use as human sacrifices in attempts to ensure good hunting.

Perhaps the guardian spirits of the children had not been strong enough or sufficiently alert to danger to prevent this mysterious disappearance. It was a local tradition that each infant was given a guardian spirit to safeguard that person throughout their life. The strongest and wisest guardians, those who had successfully protected an ancestor into old age, were reassigned to the newest members of the family. Boys received stronger guardians than girls. The sons of chiefs were awarded more powerful and more experienced guardian spirits than lower ranking families' offspring. It was believed that these guardian spirits could materialize as animals, especially during emergencies. Powerful guardian spirits would be seen as wolves, bears, or mountain lions. Eagles and hawks could be manifestations of vigilant guardians, while rabbits, squirrels, raccoons, beavers, and minks personified weaker or less experienced guardians.

Thus, the mysterious disappearances and likely deaths of the five children produced not only the ghosts of the children but the ghosts of their guardians as well. The guardian spirits, condemned by their failures to protect their charges, must wander eternally in penance for their weakness and inattention.

The phantoms of the five children, still carrying their baskets of huckleberries, occasionally can be seen on summer evenings at dusk. As ghosts of innocent children, they pose no threat to the living, whom they ignore. The guardian spirits, however, are another matter. They are likely to be aggressive toward strangers, trying desperately to redeem themselves from their tragic failures two centuries ago. They can be especially terrifying when taking physical form as a large predator-like a bear or mountain lion.

The Death Ship

Only a few old-timers in the San Juan Islands can remember hearing the legend of the death ship. Either it hasn't appeared lately or those who've witnessed it have been too traumatized to talk about it.

As recorded in surviving narratives from the past, it was an awesome and fearsome sight. The death ship appears without warning, suddenly surging out of a fog bank, usually at dusk or dawn. It is a three-masted sailing ship, with every sail unfurled but hanging slack from the yardarms, even if there is a wind. The sails are gray with age and are tattered and torn. The rope rigging is visibly frayed and rotted. The ship displays no running lights. Several skeletons can be seen aloft in the rigging, and a badly decayed corpse stands at the ship's wheel, staring straight ahead with sightless eyes. There is no sound of any kind.

The death ship makes no waves, and leaves no wake as it moves across the sea. It seems to be on a collision course with those unfortunate enough to see it, but at the last possible second, it veers off and flies by with inches to spare. Some of those who've seen the death ship report an overwhelming blast of a foul odor of decay as it passes. Some accounts claim to have seen the name "Louise" and her home port, "New Bedford," printed in faded white across her stern.

Now for the truly scary part. The legend holds that if you see the death ship, someone you know will be dead within twenty-four hours—not necessarily someone close to you, but someone known to you. The good news, according to the story, is that the death ship never appears to the person who is about to die—death likes to come unannounced.

The legend of the death ship asserts that it is the phantom of an actual ship that sank in these waters in the early 1800s, taking all aboard down with her. This tragedy was no accident.

It's been said that sailors are a superstitious lot. Theirs is a dangerous occupation, filled with perils beyond human control. Reportedly, those aboard *Louise* on her final, fatal voyage ignored or decidedly flouted many sailors' taboos. The *Louise* was a working ship, a whaler, not a passenger ship, and thus a woman aboard was considered bad luck. The captain had brought his bride with him on its last journey. He had won her affections over another ardent suitor who also happened to be the first mate of the ship, his second in command. This potentially explosive situation was worsened by the captain's unaccountable breaking with long traditions. Changing the name of a ship is considered bad luck. Christened the *Champion*, it was renamed *Louise* in honor of the captain's bride. When *Louise* left port for the last time, the captain neglected to toss a penny into the sea as a tribute to Neptune, god of the seas. If Neptune is thus ignored, say sailors, he may decide to sink the ship. The captain further challenged fate by shooting an albatross to impress his bride with his marksmanship. As every sailor believes, this is the worst folly; albatrosses are said to contain the souls of those lost at sea and must not be harassed in any way.

The *Louise* was doomed. The first mate, forced to observe the radiant happiness of the captain and his bride, who once was the first mate's betrothed, deliberately steered the ship into the rocks in a violent rage of jealousy. In effect, he murdered all aboard and committed suicide. A suicide is believed to doom a ship to become a phantom of death.

Ghostly Gasping for Breath

Drowning must rank among the worst possible ways to die. Death by drowning seldom is mercifully quick. The victim has agonizingly long minutes to anticipate his death. The body spasms while every muscle participates in an effort to breath. The terror of not being able to gulp in the life-sustaining oxygen dominates the last moments of consciousness. The victim's last frantic efforts to breathe are at last stilled. Some of the ghosts of drowning victims are eternally reliving their last moments of consciousness, faces contorted in the horror of impending death. Other ghosts in the water or on the beaches have the limp forms and sightless eyes of the recently deceased.

Ghosts of drowning victims appear in the swift currents of the narrow straits and channels around the San Juan Islands, clustered at the southern end of the Strait of Georgia and the northern end of Puget Sound. There are more than 170 islands in the San Juans, about 70 of them south of the Canadian border, which zigzags through the islands. The islands are the tips of a submerged mountain chain and are now mostly tourist destinations. Uncrowded beaches, hospitable yacht harbors, and tranquil farm scenes lure visitors. Some of the state's oldest communities host artist colonies, and whale watching is a popular activity.

But there is a dark side to the history of this seemingly idyllic corner of the Evergreen State. Those ghosts of drowning victims are restless because not only were they wrenched from life by sudden tragedy, but many were murdered. They were murdered by a grisly and pitiless combination of greed and racial discrimination. Most of them are Chinese.

Why would so many Chinese ghosts float in these waters? As in California from the 1850s through 1870s, Chinese labor, cheap and willing, began to flood into the old Oregon Territory to fill the demand for workers in a fast-growing economy. Mining, fishing, lumbering, and railroad construction all offered opportunities for Chinese immigrants. Non-Chinese laborers blamed the Chinese for keeping wages low, and serious anti-Chinese riots broke out across Washington in the mid-1880s. Federal Chinese Exclusion Acts in 1881 and 1886 severely restricted Chinese immigration. One result

was a smuggling industry transporting illegals from Canada, which was less restrictive, down the coast by boat to secluded beaches from Everett to Tacoma.

It was a very lucrative business for the smugglers, as the going price for bringing Chinese from Canada into the United States was $500 a head, payable in advance. In the 1890s that was really big money.

The most notorious smuggler was one Larry Kelly, based on Sinclair Island, one of the easternmost of the San Juan Islands. Everyone, including Customs and Immigration and the Coast Guard, knew that Kelly was smuggling Chinese down Puget Sound and into the country. They knew it, but they couldn't prove it. Kelly sailed only on dark and stormy nights. If he spotted a Coast Guard cutter, he'd throw his human cargo overboard, so that if boarded by the Coast Guard, there was no evidence of Chinese. And thus, lots of ghosts of Chinese drowning victims haunt these waters.

The Cascades

THE CASCADE RANGE, A SERIES OF GIANT VOLCANOES, RUNS NORTH-south in Washington from the Canadian border to the Columbia Gorge. This mountain spine literally divides Washington's natural environments. The Cascades and the land to the west are wet. Some places, like Snoqualmie Pass, receive more than 400 inches of snow annually, and parts of the Olympic Mountains are drenched with 400 inches of rain every year. To the east of the Cascades, some of the nation's largest irrigation projects support farming in a semi-desert land.

Supernatural tales from the Cascades include the first UFO sighting recorded in the modern era, the phantoms produced by an avalanche, and the ghostly victims of a coal mine disaster. You'll read about the Evergreen State's own Romeo and Juliet. A railroad tunnel contains some threatening spirits, and a horrendous natural disaster is foretold by a clairvoyant. Bigfoot interrupts a family camping weekend and a gracious ghost crashes the party.

The First UFO?

A Seattle pilot had a life-transforming experience high above Mount Rainier. He was part of a large number of private pilots who had volunteered to help search for a missing military transport plane.

He flew his single-engine Cessna over the magnificent volcano that serves as a symbol of Seattle. All experienced pilots keep fully aware of the skies around them, and his search-and-report mission heightened his surveillance of the area. At about mid-afternoon, he noticed a small group of strange-looking craft in formation above the mountain. They appeared to be performing aerial acrobatics, as in a flying circus. A total of nine craft zoomed in and out of the clouds, playing a high-speed game of leapfrog, diving and swooping around one another. He described them as being very shiny, reflecting the sun like silver mirrors. They were as large as a DC-4, a popular passenger carrier of the day, and were disc-like in appearance, like gigantic pie plates.

The amazed pilot then watched the objects regroup and suddenly accelerate to the south, toward Mount Adams, about 48 miles from Mount Rainier. He timed their flight from mountain to mountain, and calculated their speed at about 1,200 miles per hour. As an experienced pilot, he knew that no known piloted craft could fly that fast—after all, this was 1947, June 24 to be exact.

The pilot, Kenneth Arnold, knew that his observations were literally unbelievable, but he decided to report them anyway. A newspaper reporter invented a new descriptive phrase—"flying saucer"—when writing up Arnold's story, the very first use of this term. The story caused a sensation and attracted scornful skepticism from experts.

An Army Air Force spokesman in the Pentagon commented: "As far as we know, nothing flies that fast except a German V-2 rocket, which travels at about 3,500 miles an hour—and that's too fast to be seen." And, of course, V-2s were unmanned rockets, completely incapable of the abrupt, high-speed turns observed by Arnold.

Following closely on Arnold's sudden fame, the story and the term "flying saucer" spread around the world. UFO sightings began to flood the media. Was this some sort of mass hysteria? Were hundreds of people who might have kept silent about these weirdly impossible aircraft now emboldened by a report from a responsible professional pilot?

On July 4, 1947, only ten days after Arnold's story was reported, an off-duty coastguardsman took what may be the first photo of a flying saucer from his Lake City backyard. Was this one of the UFOs first seen by Arnold? Why would Washington State be visited by

UFOs? Were the presumed pilots of the strange craft, whether human or non-human, particularly interested in the new types of aircraft being developed by the Boeing Company?

Then, a report came in from Maine, almost 3,000 miles from Mount Rainier. A flying saucer was reported near the town of Presque Isle. Old-timers there are still divided in their opinion as to whether a genuine UFO was seen there or whether there was some other explanation for the fantastic story told by a preacher's son.

The fact that the witness was a preacher's son was used to support beliefs by both sides on this controversy. Believers in UFOs asserted that being a preacher's son and reared in a household of piety and strict observance of the Ten Commandments should make the word of this lad more reliable than most. Who but a preacher's son would be more familiar with the commandment forbidding bearing false witness? On the other hand, those inclined to doubt the UFO report from the preacher's son also cite his father's occupation as a reason for disbelief.

The Presque Isle preacher's offspring had observed, while on a solitary camping and hunting trip out in the woods, a celestial object traveling so quickly that it created its own whirling sound. It appeared from a cloud, surrounded by flashes like lightning. In the midst of a brilliant light, it glowed like molten metal. Out of this fiery sphere came four creatures that looked, at first glance, like men; however, as they got closer, it became clear that each visitor had four faces and four wings. Their legs were straight and their feet looked like cow's hooves. Under each wing they had human-like hands. These alien creatures moved straight ahead without turning as they went. Their bodies glowed with bright light as though they were on fire, but they did not burn. They could move as fast as lightning.

Fascinating, said the believers. After all, he is a preacher's son, so he wouldn't lie. Fascinating indeed, said the skeptics. They pointed out that, as a preacher's son, he would have heard or read about precisely those images in the Bible—in the first chapter of the Book of Ezekiel, to be exact.

Yes, this description does appear in Ezekiel, which brings up another question: Could the ancient Israelites, during their captivity in Babylon, have actually witnessed aliens emerging from a UFO? Read Ezekiel for yourself.

The Bible has been cited by scientists for the geographical information information it contains. Modern archeologists have used the scriptures to locate long-lost settlements and buried springs. Geologists' interpretations of biblical accounts have led to the rediscovery of mineral deposits. Maybe the account in Ezekiel is a literal report and not an allegory.

Although the 1947 event at Mount Rainier led to an immediate rash of alleged sightings around the world, people actually may have seen UFOs long before the term was coined. When reviewing some old stories about mysterious experiences, the possibility of long-ago UFO encounters arises.

For example, in the early 1800s, the clipper ship *Goodspeed* was making her way along the Maine coast on a voyage from Halifax to Portland. It was a calm, starry night with a northeast wind filling her sails and guaranteeing a speedy arrival in port within a day or two. The night watch was uneventful—that is, until a "very bright light, spinning like a child's top, suddenly soared over the tall masts." The mysterious object, "glowing like molten iron," didn't make a sound as it circled the ship. It "hovered above us like a hawk riding the air currents," reported the helmsman, then suddenly it accelerated and quickly disappeared from sight.

When the *Goodspeed*'s crew told their story to others, it was considered just another tall tale, a product of too much rum and too much imagination. Did those long-ago sailors have an encounter with what we would call a UFO? Or did they just make up a good story to earn a few free drinks in a waterfront tavern?

Maybe the UFO stories of the modern world started in the Evergreen State, or perhaps these mysterious visitors have appeared since Biblical times. Who can say for certain?

A Clairvoyant's Vision of Disaster

The nightmares came every night. They were similar, like minor variations on a theme. It seemed as though the same horrific events were being seen from different viewpoints, over and over again.

The dreams invariably began with the ground shaking. Wavelike ripples appeared to move across solid ground, a most unsettling experience. The sound of a tremendous explosion accompanied the quake. A massive cloud of black dust appeared over the distant mountain, creating a darkness at noon. Then a distant rumbling sound could be heard, rapidly growing louder as though a freight train was bearing down on this listener. The ground seemed to be moving again, this time trembling rather than shaking.

Then the most fearful phase of the nightmare began. A huge wave of mud and debris moves downslope, sweeping over anything in its path—trees, cars, large pieces of buildings, carcasses of cattle and deer—all are carried along in a thick gumbo of mud. Panicked people trying to flee the swiftly advancing tide are overwhelmed, their screams cut short as they are dragged down into the churning muck.

In the dream, the badly frightened observer is running full tilt up the valley wall now, legs pumping furiously, lungs on fire, heart pumping frantically in the escape attempt. But it is no use—the muddy wave hits with the force of an NFL lineman, and the victim is pulled down into the reeking morass. It is at this point that the dreamer awakes, drenched as usual in cold, oily sweat, heart pounding as though it's about to burst out of the chest, legs twitching furiously as though still racing away from certain death.

After suffering through this recurring nightmare for weeks, the desperate dreamer consulted a psychic of her mother's acquaintance. The psychic listened carefully to her story and advised the young woman, whom we'll call Liz, that she was most likely experiencing episodes of clairvoyance. *Clairvoyance*, French for "clear seeing," is an extrasensory perception that often overlaps with telepathy and precognition, knowledge of the future, or even retrocognition, paranormal insight into the past. Historically, individuals gifted with clairvoyance, also called "second sight" or "ghost vision," have been called prophets, witches, and wizards. Many people believe, however, that everyone possesses a capacity for clairvoyance and may experience one or two such episodes in their lives.

The psychic believed that the strong persistence of Liz's visions suggested clairvoyance, rather than mere nightmares. Could the scenario of a massive mudflow possibly happen in reality? Talk with a geologist or physical geographer to learn if such phenomena occur in the physical world, was the psychic's advice. The answer is a clear, certain, and truly frightening yes, it can and it has. Could it happen again?

Mount Rainier was the culprit. This beloved icon of Seattle, whose citizens simply call it "the Mountain," is at least half a million years old. At more than 14,400 feet high, its mass ranks it among the largest volcanoes in the world. Rainier seems to loom over Seattle, 54 miles away. Geologists believe that, five thousand years ago, the volcano was more than 16,000 feet tall, but that its top was blown off in a tremendous explosion. Just as today, its peak would have been covered in thick ice and snow, which instantly melted in the heat of the explosion. The pulverized rock combined with melt water to form a huge mudflow, called a *lahar*. The lahar of approximately five thousand years ago reached Puget Sound. Tacoma and south Seattle are built atop this ancient mudflow. A more recent explosion and mudflow occurred about 530 years ago, covering ground now occupied by Enumclaw, Orting, Kent, Auburn, and most of Renton. About 150,000 people now live atop this smaller mudflow's remnants. If a similar explosion were to happen again, the resulting mudflow would be directed by gravity and terrain over the same land again.

While another cataclysmic eruption is not considered imminent, Rainier is far from dead. An average of thirty minor earthquakes a year shake the mountain. Escaping steam from underground has created a warm-water lake under 100 feet of ice near the summit. Is Mount Rainier trying to tell us something? Were Liz's dreams really clairvoyant glimpses of the future? Liz, incidentally, has since moved to Kansas.

Buried Alive

Fortunately for everyone's sanity and composure, this particular phantom's appearances have become rare. Perhaps, after a century and a quarter, this horribly traumatized soul has at last found peace.

A longtime resident of Gold Bar, who has asked not to be identified, may have been among the last to witness this particular ghost. The figure was that of a middle-aged Chinese man. He is dressed in loose-fitting trousers and tunic of dark blue cotton and wears a traditional long braid of hair down his back. His face, which appears to be coated with dark earth, is contorted in an agonizing grimace, a silent scream. His fingers are frozen in a clawing position, the nails torn and bleeding. After struggling mightily to stand upright, the figure falls backwards into the grave it was trying to escape. The peace of the small, derelict cemetery is one again undisturbed.

Stunned and badly frightened, the observer decided to tell no one of this horrifying experience. Gradually, however, he learned that this apparition has been recorded by other local people, and that the story dates back to the 1880s.

Gold Bar was named by an overly optimistic prospector who found traces of gold in a small stream. A major strike never followed, despite frantic activity by men dreaming of finding their fortune. They tried, but only small amounts of the precious metal rewarded their sweat, only sufficient to keep them digging.

Then the little community got a second lease on life. The Great Northern Railway chose a route through Gold Bar for its transcontinental line across the Cascades. Gold Bar made a transition from a rough-and-tumble mining town to an even rougher and more violent construction camp, or shanty town as they were called. The railroad workers were infamously hardworking, hard-drinking, and hard-playing. Their shanty towns were lawless collections of saloons, gambling houses, and brothels, frequently all in one establishment.

Gunfights were common for any reason, or no reason. Being accused of cheating at cards, founded or unfounded, was akin to a death sentence, as was failure to fill a whiskey glass to the brim. Racial animosity toward Chinese laborers, imported by the railroad as construction workers, exploded in race riots. Gangs of well-armed white men were organized to hunt down and kill Chinese.

"The only way a Chinaman leaves Gold Bar is in a coffin," boasted a drunken gang leader. This inspired the local construction boss for the Great Northern to order the local undertaker's shop to hastily assemble a lot of coffins. He would save lives by shipping his Chinese employees out of town hidden in coffins. This worked, except for one last Chinese man. Running out of coffins, the undertaker persuaded the terrified man to lie atop a corpse already in the last coffin. He gave the poor man a large glass of whiskey and advised him to "play dead" if anyone opened the coffin, scheduled for burial the next day. An extremely unfortunate misunderstanding led to that coffin being buried later that same day by an eager new assistant.

The terror of awakening in a buried coffin, lying atop a real corpse, can only be imagined. The man struggled frantically in the tight confines of the coffin, eventually succumbing to lack of oxygen. His traumatized spirit repeated this claustrophobic horror at every full moon, so the story goes.

The Tunnel's Supernatural Threats

There was a time when hikers and bikers could travel through a disused railroad tunnel at Snoqualmie Pass. Now they can't, at least not legally. That might be just as well according to some who believe they've sensed dangers of the supernatural variety in the tunnel.

Snoqualmie Pass, 3,022 feet above sea level, has been used to cross the Cascades for as long as people have lived here. An Indian trail followed this pass, eventually replaced by a pioneer wagon trail, then a railroad, and now Interstate 90.

The 2.3-mile-long railroad tunnel was built between 1908 and 1911. It was one of the longest rail tunnels in the world at that time. In the 1970s, the ceiling of the tunnel was raised to accommodate double-stacked container cars, a project that may have resurrected the dark forces that infest the tunnel.

Following the bankruptcy of the railroad in 1980, the state took control of the tunnel and made it part of Iron Horse State Park, a popular hiking and biking trail. Snoqualmie Pass Tunnel was closed in 2009 because of falling rocks, which the state could not afford to clear. Although the tunnel is drilled through solid rock, natural fractures in the rock create zones of instability in the ceiling. And then there is the supernatural instability of the underworld.

Those who work underground always are aware of the dangers this entails. It is a little nerve-racking to remember that thousands of tons of rock are overhead and could collapse in at any moment. Using explosives to aid in digging amplifies the danger. Add in the threats of insufficient oxygen and noxious gases, and working underground becomes one of the most dangerous occupations possible.

People engaged in particularly dangerous occupations often develop a set of superstitions and beliefs in dark forces beyond their control. Tunnels and mines are, after all, spooky places, lit only by flickering torches or a few feeble lamps. Odd echoes bounce off rock walls and ceilings. It is easy to believe in the presence or influence of unseen forces.

It is said that Native Americans were astonished that their white neighbors were foolish enough to go underground at all, much less work underground for whole days. Several Native American tribes believe that the literal underworld was the domain of evil, while the sky was the domain of positive energies and goodness. Someone burrowing into the earth was certain to encounter and challenge the forces of evil.

Miners and other underground workers believe that mines and tunnels are inhabited by impish, troublemaking little people. The Tommyknockers, mysterious creatures, were more inclined to non-lethal mischief, while other, darker supernatural forces threatened mayhem and death. The Tommyknockers could be placated, but life-threatening powers were thought to be omnipresent and all-powerful.

When the Snoqualmie Tunnel was open, hikers and bikers often retreated in near panic, convinced that they were being harassed or threatened by ghosts or demons. Strangely glowing misty forms appeared. Odd whispers hinted at gruesome events forthcoming, and showers of stones pelted them from the walls and ceiling. Even if the tunnel is reopened to the public eventually, it might be a good idea to not again enter the realm of the Tommyknockers.

The Death Train

The huge steam locomotive, one of the largest ever built, climbs the steep grade leading into the tunnel. Its massive drive wheels power a short train of old-fashioned passenger cars, all lit brilliantly within. A scattering of passengers occupy some of the dark blue plush seats. They seem to stare fixedly straight ahead, ignoring both the spectacular scenery and one another. Great puffs of black coal smoke billow from the locomotive's smokestack, and wisps of steam escape the cylinders at the ends of the driving rods. The bright headlight shines into the entrance of the Stampede Tunnel. One by one, the passenger cars labeled "Northern Pacific Railroad" disappear into the two-mile long tunnel.

It is a scene right out of the Pacific Northwest's history. This type of train no longer crosses the Cascades. The Northern Pacific long ago was absorbed into the Burlington Northern Santa Fe, and the massive steam locomotives built specifically to handle the long, steep grades through the Cascades are gone. The Stampede Tunnel itself sat vacant between 1984 and 1992, the period when eyewitnesses claim to have seen the death train entering or leaving the tunnel. The tunnel is back in use, enlarged to accommodate modern double-deck intermodal cars.

The reports of those who've seen the phantom death train agree about several points. The train itself is an anachronism—the locomotive and cars date to the late nineteenth century and are not seen outside of museums. The train makes no sound at all as it steams past. The death train earned its name because its passengers appear to consist entirely of the recently deceased. One eyewitness claims to have recognized a neighbor looking sightlessly out the window, no expression or recognition on her face. On reaching home, the observer was told that the neighbor had died around the time that she had been seen aboard the phantom train. Does the death train carry souls on their final journey to the next world?

If the ghostly train is a death train, the Stampede Tunnel is an appropriate place for it to appear. The building of the tunnel took more than two years and cost at least thirty-one lives. The tunnel has no daylight visible in the center; it is arched, not a straight-line bore. Thus the tunnel of darkness is also a tunnel of death traversed on occasion by the supernatural train.

The Shades of Monte Christo

The good news is that the scenic highway between Darrington and Granite Falls, all fifty-five miles of it, is open again after having been closed repeatedly by flood damage. This opens up some truly spectacular areas of scenic wilderness, including the ghost town of Monte Christo.

Monte Christo is a ghost town in two senses. It is the shadow of a once-thriving mining town. Nothing much is left except a few crumbling foundations and some gaping holes where miners once labored to produce gold and silver. Monte Christo also is a town populated by ghosts. These ghosts are more likely to be heard than seen, although they still appear to some hikers and campers in the vicinity.

Monte Christo, like many small mining communities, lived a brief but frantic existence. Founded in 1889, Monte Christo hit its peak in the mid-1890s, with a population reaching two thousand and a daily train to and from Everett. Gold and silver strikes brought in many eager fortune seekers. Some made money in the mines, while others made money off the miners. Seven saloons were complemented by four gambling and dance halls, all mining gold and silver from miners' pockets. While the boom lasted, Monte Christo was a raucous and colorful little town, but by 1900, the gold and silver production was petering out. The railroad stopped running in 1903. The town was completely abandoned by 1933; the railroad tracks were torn up for scrap in 1936. Present roads follow the old right-of-way.

Following the old adage that the best place to look for gold is near where it's been found before, prospectors have since wandered around the remnants of Monte Christo, trying their luck and trying to ignore the ghosts. Many agree that the ghosts are out there. They've been seen and they've been heard.

The sounds of picks and shovels striking hard rock frequently can be heard coming from long-abandoned mines. This would be less surprising if it wasn't in the dead of night. And then there are the sounds of merriment—ragtime piano, clinking glasses, and drunken laughter—coming from the ruins of what once must have been saloons and dance halls.

Recently, two hikers reported a somewhat unnerving experience near the site of Monte Christo. As they emerged from the forest into a small clearing, they saw a grizzled old-timer standing next to a heavily laden packhorse. The white-bearded, raggedly dressed man did not look happy to see them. In fact, he was pointing a rifle at them. "Why are you following me?" he challenged them. "Are you hoping that I'll lead you to my strike?" The terrified duo hastened to reassure the gun-toting stranger that they were just out enjoying nature. "Well, if I was you, I'd stay real still for a while" was the old prospector's advice. The hikers followed the advice religiously— except for some quite understandable trembling—as the old man and his horse just evaporated like a morning mist.

Other campers reported seeing luminous, almost transparent, forms gliding through the old town site around midnight. The figures appear to be those of an assortment of dancehall girls, miners, and gunslingers. These phantoms do not attempt to interact with the living, unlike the old prospector.

Washington's Own Romeo and Juliet

The sublime tragedy of Shakespeare's timeless masterpiece, *Romeo and Juliet,* is that the young lovers' deaths were so needless. In the classic play, Romeo commits suicide believing that Juliet is dead, not knowing that she was merely in a drugged deep sleep. An awakening Juliet, seeing her lover's dead body, then commits suicide herself. Lack of communication led to a double tragedy. They truly were "star-crossed lovers."

The Evergreen State's history has its very own star-crossed lovers, and this tragedy produced two heart-wrenching ghosts. The tiny community of Index is located on scenic US Route 2. Whitewater rafting and back-country trekking are popular activities for the many tourists who are attracted by the spectacular views. Many stay at the renowned Bush House Country Inn, famous for its gracious hospitality. The Bush House also is famous for its ghosts. These particular spirits never threaten or deliberately scare people. They appear only occasionally, always unobtrusively and always pitiable.

The Bush House was built in 1898 to host miners and quarry workers in the area. In 1900, a lovely young woman, Annabel, came to the town to marry her lover, a miner by trade. It was a joyful time. Annabel brought her wedding gown with her, happily anticipating the ceremony that would follow their reunion. The couple had postponed their wedding until he could save up enough money from his job. After a passionate greeting, the miner left to work a double shift to earn his holiday bonus. "I'll see you tomorrow my darling," he said. "I'm looking forward to our first dance as man and wife."

A massive explosion broke the early-morning stillness. The whole town raced to the mine. Smoke and choking rock dust filled the air. The scene was chaotic as would-be rescuers began digging through the debris that blocked the mine entrance. A terrified and bewildered Annabel joined the wives and children milling about the mine, frantic for news, weeping, and praying. Before noon, a mine official posted a list of men missing and presumed dead. Annabel's lover was on the list.

Heartbroken, Annabel stumbled back to the Bush House, barely able to see through her tears. Suddenly and tragically her world was turned upside down. In a few hours, she had gone from a radiantly happy bride-to-be to a mournful survivor, all hopes of happiness and fulfillment smashed. Thoroughly distraught, Annabel carefully brushed her hair, applied her makeup, and donned her wedding dress. Then she hanged herself in her room.

It was her lover who discovered her lifeless though still warm body hanging from the ceiling light. He instantly realized what had happened. Unhurt in the explosion, he heroically volunteered to stay in the mine to aid in the rescue attempt. His name had mistakenly been added to the list of those missing.

Unable to face life without him, Annabel had committed suicide. Her tear-stained note said that she had come to join her beloved "in the pure light of heaven." Her lover decided to join her; he shot himself in the head. They were buried in the same grave.

But their spirits returned from the grave to haunt the Bush House. They have been seen as an almost transparent couple, waltzing to unheard music. She is wearing her wedding gown and he is in his new dark suit. They are smiling at each other, united for all eternity, just like Shakespeare's star-crossed lovers.

The Spirits of Spirit Lake

Spirit Lake, not surprisingly, is filled with spirits, or so the local Native Americans believe. A great many people of all races and ethnic backgrounds agree that Spirit Lake is aptly named. It is a spooky place and has been for many centuries.

Spirit Lake lies only about seven miles northeast of Mount St. Helens, and their geological histories and mysterious powers are connected. The lake, according to geologists, was created long ago by the eruption of the great volcano. Lava rock and cinders ejected from Mount St. Helens buried an entire forest and dammed a stream, creating the lake. This theorized origin was proven correct when the

1980 eruption, which shot a dense plume of smoke and ash 80,000 feet in the air, released an avalanche of debris a mile wide, raising the lake's surface by another two hundred feet. Spirit Lake reaches astonishing depths. Many spots are more than 1,300 feet deep. These mysterious depths may be one reason for the lake's supernatural aura. Who knows what might exist at such depths?

According to tribal traditions, Spirit Lake is the home of many spirits—some good, some evil, many violent, and a few capable of predicting the future. It is these spirit prophets who may be the most important phantoms; their messages and warnings are said to foretell disaster.

The vicinity of Spirit Lake is noted for weird sounds. The very earth seems to whisper and moan. The reason for these phenomena may be the unusual terrain produced by past volcanic eruptions. As great flows of hot liquid rock poured down the mountain thousands of years ago, the top crust cooled solid while molten lava continued to drain from beneath it. This led to long, winding lava tubes or underground tunnels. One, Ape Cave, is more than 12,000 feet long, with many side branches. Air currents in these lava tubes can make it seem as though the earth itself is breathing, sighing, whispering, and moaning.

Local legend has it that these sounds are caused by *siatcoes*, outcast spirits from other tribes who have the power to speak through various animals or even trees and rocks. These supernatural ventriloquists sometimes deliver urgent warnings to the living when the mountain may again explode and destroy all life around it.

Another old tradition is that a giant elk lured a young brave out hunting food for his starving family many centuries ago. The elk led the hunter into the lake and then drowned him. To this day, according to myth, the huge elk and his pursuer appear at the lake when an eruption is near. The elk and hunter were spotted just before May 18, 1980, when an incredible explosion tore the top 1,300 feet off the mountain, scattering ash over parts of three states. It could happen again at any time.

Victims of the White Death

Driving across the Cascade Range in a snowstorm can be an unnerving experience, one made infinitely more frightening if you catch a brief glimpse of the Snow People, victims of the White Death. These Snow People are not the smiley sculptures built by children in backyards, quite the opposite. They are the ghosts of a disaster that long ago killed 118 people.

The specters of the Snow People haven't been reported as much recently as in the past. Some experts in psychic phenomena believe the diminishing appearances indicate that the dead have at last accepted their fates and moved on to the next world. Others are of the opinion that many of those who have seen them have, consciously or unconsciously, refused to accept what their senses tell them, so unbelievably horrific and pitiful are these supernatural images.

The shocked witnesses see men, women, and children covered in frost lurching through the snow by the side of the road. There are dozens, even scores, of them. Dead, dark eyes stare out of faces frozen in expressions of horrified disbelief. Crusts of snow and ice cling to old-fashioned woolen coats and hats. Icicles drip from eyebrows, noses, and ears. The figures stumble along as though compelled to move, blindly wandering through the storm, for they most often are seen only during whiteouts. The severely limited visibility during a whiteout doubtlessly contributes to the small number of reported sightings. Certainly, some will conclude that it is better for their mental health to decide that these are just storm-induced images.

As mountaineers and skiers know, avalanches are the White Death of snow-covered mountains. Hundreds of thousands of tons of snow, accumulated on steep slopes, can suddenly break loose and slide down the mountains, reaching impressive speeds and destroying and burying anything in their path. Annual snowfall totals in the Cascade Range can average between 300 to 400 inches, so avalanches there are not uncommon.

The specific White Death that allegedly produced the ghostly snow people occurred on March 2, 1910. A passenger train had been stalled in deep snow at the western portal of the old Cascade tunnel at a tiny railroad station called Wellington. The train was snowbound here from February 22 through March 2, when a massive avalanche swept the train and station down to the bottom of a 400-foot-deep canyon. Those who didn't suffocate died a lingering death by freezing. Only a handful of passengers survived. The phantoms of people, it is said, still wander whenever blizzards call them back to the scene of their tragic and untimely deaths.

The Gracious Guest

She is the epitome of the gracious guest—a smiling, respectful, considerate, and quiet participant in the festivities. She is self-effacing, never competing for the focus of attention that rightfully belongs to the bride, the birthday celebrant, or the guest of honor. She's not much for conversation; in fact, she's never uttered a word so far as anyone can remember.

Many who have briefly glimpsed the gracious guest remember only a sweet smile, a wordless salute with a wine glass, or an elegant wave of greeting and approval. Very few know that they've seen a ghost, unless they tried to approach her, when the unknown guest disappears before their eyes.

She appears always on the fringe of the group. Visually, she is on the edge of one's attention. She is most often described in rather vague terms, as though the observer never really paid much interest in her, clearly focusing elsewhere. She is said to be a genteel lady in her seventies, tastefully dressed in pink. She is not seen eating, but often holds a wine glass, which may be just a prop to explain her silence. This particular ghost appears occasionally at Alexander's Country Inn and Restaurant, located in Ashford, a mile from the southeast entrance to Mount Rainier National Park. Alexander's is one of Washington's oldest country inns, dating to 1912. The spectacular views of the majestic peak are complemented by luxurious accommodations and a gourmet restaurant, and of course, the delightfully mysterious and unobtrusive spirit of the gracious guest. Who is she, or rather, who was she? What is she doing there? No one knows the answers. Obviously, she enjoys being at Alexander's, at least in spirit.

The Tragic Ghosts of Roslyn

It has been observed that people engaged in highly dangerous occupations often develop a fatalistic view of life and can become very superstitious. Mine disasters have a way of reinforcing miners' traditions concerning luck. While Washington is not commonly identified as a coal-mining state, it does have coal, mining, and tragically, the ghosts of coal miners.

Mining has produced a lot of legends and miners' superstitions, as well as tragic deaths. Underground mines always have been dangerous places to work. It takes courage to work daily with an entire mountain looming above your head. Foul air and toxic gases can kill as well, and on top of all this, inadequate ventilation can allow dangerous buildups of coal dust, which can explode when introduced to a tiny spark. Fires, once started, can burn for decades, sucking up all available oxygen. Tunnel collapses can trap miners deep beneath the surface, sentencing them to painfully slow deaths by suffocation.

Most miners were hardworking, hard-playing, and very superstitious. Miners have learned to pay attention to hunches, or vague feelings of impending disaster. Many a miner has suddenly decided to run out of a mine, only to have a sudden cave-in or explosion destroy the tunnel he'd just vacated.

Mines can be pretty spooky places—almost total darkness lit by a few feeble flickering lamps. Odd echoes bounce off the rock walls and ceilings. Imagination works overtime. Most of the old-time miners believed that the mines were inhabited by impish, troublemaking "little people." The German-born miners called them *Kobolds*; the Mexicans called them *Duendes*. To the English, they were the Tommyknockers. These mysterious creatures most often were inclined to mischief rather than life-threatening foul play. They would hide tools and play pranks on the miners. Miners used to leave offerings of food to keep them in good humor. In a mine, any small mishap can and will be blamed on the Tommyknockers.

Miners in the old days were convinced that bad things happened in threes. An accident would be followed quickly by two more. Accidents were most frequent around midnight. A woman in a mine brought bad luck. If a miner's lamp flickered or went dim, that meant his woman was seeing another man.

Mine rats must never be harmed. Killing a mine rat underground would be like killing a dog above ground. Mine rats are believed to be able to sense the slightest movement in the rock and will scamper to safety before a cave-in, thus warning miners to do the same. The mine rats, accordingly, are fed food scraps and encouraged to hang around. In May 1892, Washington's worst coal mine disaster occurred in the tiny town of Roslyn. The Northern Pacific Railroad had opened a mine there in 1886. While many early locomotives in the West burned wood, the Northern Pacific's engines needed the much higher energy content of coal to power up the long grades of the Cascades.

Sometimes, the restless spirits of those who died in agonizing terror manifest in the world of the living as sounds rather than as visible apparitions. So it is with the forty-five victims of the disaster at Roslyn. Ever since then, many people have reported hearing the sound of tortured, strangled gasping for breath, punctuated by hoarse screams for help. Surely slow suffocation, trapped far underground, is one of the most excruciating deaths anyone could suffer. As the available oxygen is used up, the victim becomes ever more aware of the desperation of the situation and the inevitability of his or her fate. The chest muscles expand the lungs in a frantic though hopeless attempt to gain sufficient air. Eventually, the oxygen-starved brain begins to shut down, and the helpless victim loses consciousness. Imagine hearing your workmates and friends around you gasping their last breaths, knowing that you will soon follow them in death.

When rescue crews finally broke through the debris-clogged collapsed tunnels to reach the trapped miners, they were all dead. It was reported that the would-be rescuers recoiled in horror when they saw the agonized grimaces on the victims' faces. They had soul-wrenching nightmares about those tortured faces for the rest of their lives.

To this day, as dusk approaches each May evening, some hear the faint sounds of protracted, painful gasping for breath amid the quiet of the little valley, as the pitiful spirits of the dead miners apparently relive their last hopeless, agonizing moments of life.

With nearly ten percent of its total workforce killed in one horrific day, the Northern Pacific was blamed, fairly or unfairly, for lax safety standards. In 1898, the state prohibited railroads from operating coal mines, although a second mine explosion killed ten men at Roslyn in 1909 despite different ownership.

The Wheezing Spirits

Only a few miles separate the coal-mining towns of Ravensdale and Black Diamond. Ravensdale was the site of another mine disaster. In 1915, an explosion in a mine killed thirty-one men. It is said that these victims haunt the local cemetery and are a particularly gruesome sight. These phantoms rise from their graves on moonlit nights and stagger about the headstones in an everlasting search for their missing body parts. Legless, armless, and sometimes headless torsos lurch around, seeking reunion with their missing body parts, evidently unable to rest until complete. The massive explosion that took their lives produced a gory horror of dismembered and decapitated bodies. Long before DNA could be used to match up the pieces, bodies were reassembled without any knowledge of which parts actually belonged together in a rush to give them decent burials. This postmortem chaos seems to have produced a continuing scavenger hunt among the distressed sprits of the dead.

In contrast are the pitiful, wheezing phantoms that allegedly patrol the Black Diamond Cemetery. There, late into the night, bobbing lights from miners' lamps can be seen moving among the tombstones. These eerie lights actually are small gas jets backed by polished metal reflectors worn on their hats, just as were used by miners a century ago. The flames were fed by a flammable gas produced by adding water to carbide pellets in a small tin box. The small, flickering lights are accompanied by the unnerving sound of men struggling desperately for breath.

These men died slowly, victims of silicosis, otherwise known as black lung disease. Years, even decades, of a worsening struggle for oxygen first disabled, then finally killed these luckless miners. Many years of working underground in poorly ventilated mines had clogged the miners' lungs with tiny particles of coal and rock dust. As the disease progressed, its victims' blood oxygen levels declined, robbing them of energy. Life became a frantic struggle for breath. Unable to work, unable to do anything physical, and even unable to sleep peacefully, these silicosis-cursed men died of excruciatingly slow strangulation. Their deaths were foretold by their heavy and noisy wheezing. They knew that they were doomed years before their final agonizing gasp.

Bigfoot Likes Marshmallows

They might have expected to see Bigfoot. After all, the area they were camping in was called Ape Canyon. Ape Canyon got its name from an alleged encounter with Bigfoot back in 1924. In that year, Fred Beck and three other men were staking a mining claim in an area east of Mount St. Helens. Back in the second half of the nineteenth century, gold had been found at several locations in the Cascades. Beck and his friends were simply following an old rule of miners: The best place to look for gold is where it has already been found.

As the story goes, the would-be miners noticed some very large footprints in the area in which they were prospecting. The eighteen-inch-long prints resembled those of a bear, but bears that big were not known to exist. All the men, impressed by the thought of a giant bear, decided to keep vigilant and have their rifles handy at all times. One day, they spotted a large, hairy creature, standing on two legs, watching them from behind a tree. One of Beck's companions fired, apparently missing it. The animal fled, running on two legs. While bears will rear up on their hind legs, both to get a better view and to appear more threatening, they do not run on two feet. Shortly after, several of the creatures attacked the miners' crude cabin with rocks. Later, Beck saw a similar creature standing on the rim of a canyon. He shot at the animal and seemed to have hit it, knocking it over the edge and into the canyon, known afterward as Ape Canyon.

Most stories about Bigfoot agree that the creature is curious about people but not hostile. In most accounts, when people notice the beast, it simply walks away, purposely, but not in a panic. The Beck party's experience was most unusual in that there was an attack; however, the miners had literally fired the first shot.

In 1978, the campers knew nothing of the history of Ape Canyon until later, but they are convinced that they saw Bigfoot. They wish to remain anonymous, so we'll call them the Jacksons, brothers and nephews.

The Jacksons had that uncomfortable feeling that they were being watched long before they actually spotted Bigfoot. That such a large animal as Bigfoot could remain hidden to its human neighbors should not be surprising. It is testimony to Bigfoot's intelligence and natural wariness about people. The experiences of anthropologists attempting to study chimpanzees in their natural habitats in Africa is instructive. Even though the scientists knew for certain that they were in areas populated by bands of chimps, they saw none at all for weeks. When they finally saw chimps, it was not because the anthropologists had become better trackers, they surmised. It was because the chimps had observed the intruders carefully from hiding for weeks and concluded that these humans were no threats. The chimps then simply stopped bothering to hide or run. It is likely that Bigfoot similarly is seldom careless about being spotted.

Before actually seeing Bigfoot, the Jacksons were very much aware of a powerful, eye-watering stench of unknown origin. It was, said one, like eating rotten onions in a poorly ventilated outhouse—only worse.

Then there was the puzzle of the missing marshmallows. As recommended in bear country, all food was bagged and hung high in a tree so as not to attract the interest of bears. The younger boy, however, had a private stash of marshmallows hidden in his sleeping bag. Following an afternoon of hiking, when the party returned to camp, the marshmallows were gone. The sleeping bag had not been clawed or damaged in any way, so a bear was not the culprit. Chipmunks? No, they don't carefully unzip closed-up sleeping bags. Large, opposable thumbs seemed to be indicated.

Finally, that evening, as the campers relaxed around the fire, they suddenly noticed two eyes reflecting the firelight from nearby bushes. In approved "repel the bear" fashion, they immediately yelled and pounded pots and pans. The creature turned and ran. Impulsively, the men grabbed flashlights and gave chase in the deepening dusk. They saw, very briefly, a seven-foot-tall, ape-like animal, covered in coarse dark hair, running quickly on two legs. In a flash, it was gone. Fearing ridicule, the Jacksons did not go public with this experience until decades later. Could they now revisit the scene of their experiences? Unfortunately, that entire area was devastated by the 1980 eruption of nearby Mount St. Helens. The Jacksons often wonder if "their" Bigfoot was able to survive that cataclysm.

Is Bigfoot real and still out there? If it is, don't shoot it, at least not in Skanamia County, which includes the Mount St. Helens area. County ordinance 69-01 reads, in part, "any premeditated, willful and wanton slaying of any such creature (Sasquatch) shall be deemed a felony punishable by a fine not to exceed ten thousand dollars and/or imprisonment for a period not to exceed five years." This ordinance was passed on April 1, 1969, or April Fools' Day.

Northeast Washington

THIS REGION OCCUPIES THE NORTHEASTERN QUADRANT OF WASHINGTON to the east of the Cascades and north of Interstate 90, although it includes the vicinity of Spokane. The big city is Spokane; other towns include Wenatchee and Ephrata.

This large region includes the famed Grand Coulee Dam, which is featured in the tale of intergalactic tourists aboard a UFO. The spirit of an internationally famous entertainer makes a supernatural cameo appearance, and a mysterious monster is said to lurk in the dark depths of Lake Chelan. A sacred cave hides supernatural secrets and a ghost is called upon to discipline an unruly spirit. The spirits of some rowdy pioneers show up and a ghostly messenger delivers a death notice. You'll learn about a tombstone with fatal powers and a deceased woman who helps an heir locate her missing fortune.

The Grand Tour

The Grand Coulee Dam is one of the Evergreen State's leading tourist attractions. When it was completed in 1941, it was the largest manmade structure in the world. It still ranks as one of the largest concrete structures ever built. A full mile long, the massive dam is 550 feet high, so that water cascading over its spillway is three times higher than Niagara Falls. Guided tours are popular and tourists are lured by a thirty-six minute laser light show projected onto the dam's massive facade during the summer season. The tourists love it, especially those from outer space.

Ever since construction began, in 1933, there have been rumors of nocturnal visits from mysterious aircraft. Few among the eight thousand construction workers on the dam were bold enough to talk about these UFOs, because it was clear that such talk would result in dismissal. Tight security around the dam during World War II also discouraged any interest in the occasional sightings of weird objects in the sky. Assuming that, as many believe, the UFOs are of nonterrestrial origin, why are aliens interested in the dam?

First, the dimensions of the Grand Coulee Dam make it easy to spot from very far away. If alien life forms are curious about us, and our engineering capabilities, they would be attracted to this site. Secondly, UFOs seem to be attracted to large power-generating sites—they may be somehow tapping into electrical force fields. Third, just as people enjoy tours of exotic cultures and unique natural environments, why wouldn't aliens from outer space be interested in tours of other planets or the solar systems?

A family of tourists from Massachusetts recently became firm believers in the outer-space tourism theory of UFO visitations. They related their experiences only on the grounds of anonymity. We'll call them the Adamses. They had decided to camp alongside Franklin D. Roosevelt Lake, the 150-mile-long body of water behind the Grand Coulee Dam. They found a pleasant campsite just off Route 25 on the east bank of the lake. It was mid-June, early in the season, and they were quite alone. They planned to rent a boat the next day, so they had planned a quiet evening and early bedtime. Some cold six-packs added to the relaxation around the campfire. What happened next was like a dream. Maybe it was a dream, one in which they all somehow shared.

As reported later, each person suddenly became aware of a huge dark shape hovering above them, blocking out the stars. Columns of purplish glowing light descended from the craft, about fifty feet over their heads. Each person was enveloped in their own column of light, which felt like a warm, oily substance surrounding them. Each in turn was slowly drawn up into the craft. They fell into a trancelike state, in which they seemed to share fragmentary dreams of soaring and floating over a tour of the entire length of Lake Roosevelt, the dam, and the storage reservoir called Banks Lake, then all the way to spectacular Dry Falls. They were then taken back to their campsite, where they were gently deposited back by the campfire. They believe that their whole experience lasted only a few minutes.

The Mellowest Ghost

Some people believe that a ghost makes regular visits to the student center at Spokane's Gonzaga University. This spirit, like the once-living man it represents, is friendly and easygoing—not in the least threatening or annoying. If a ghost can be described as mellow, it's this one.

The alleged ghost is thought to be that of Harry Lillis "Bing" Crosby, and the haunted place is the Crosbyana Room in the Crosby Student Center at the university. Bing Crosby's spirit is said to manifest itself mostly through sound, not sight, although a few claim to have seen him as a faintly shimmering image. Considering that Bing achieved worldwide fame as a singer, it may be a little surprising that his spirit makes itself known not by singing but by playing the drums. Drums and Bing's experience at Gonzaga University are closely linked, however.

Gonzaga's renowned law school is one of only three in the whole state. Bing enrolled there to pursue a legal career. Always interested in music, he ordered a set of drums through the mail, and he soon organized a band on the campus. The drummer and his band became very successful, especially after the drummer started doing the vocals. Almost singlehandedly, Bing developed the "crooner" style of pop music, with a soothing, easy-listening approach to romantic ballads. Bing's singing style and public persona both defined mellow—relaxed, warm, unassuming, and at the same time sophisticated. His band, which began as a casual, part-time hobby, soon became a demanding, full-time job. Bing left school in his final year, already a success in show business. Bing's experience at Gonzaga was a very positive one, however, and he became the university's most generous supporter. Gonzaga, in turn, awarded him an honorary doctorate in 1937.

Bing Crosby went on to achieve great success for himself in both music and movies. In 1944, he won a Best Actor Oscar for his role in the year's Best Picture, *Going My Way*. He starred in more than thirty films, including the seven "Road" comedies with Bob Hope. It was as a vocalist, however, that he reached international stardom. His recordings have sold an estimated half a billion copies around the world. His classic version of "White Christmas" has sold 100 million copies and was the best-selling record of all time for fifty years.

While his rival crooner, Frank Sinatra, held a "bad boy" appeal, Bing had an image of affable respectability as a loyal husband, doting father, and regular churchgoer. Bing often entertained troops close to World War II battlefields; his records were featured on armed services radio programs, which attracted German listeners as well. Among German soldiers, he was called "Der Bingle."

Bing Crosby's final live concert was given only days before his death at the age of seventy-four. Some friends believe that he was a little distressed that his voice's clarity and effortless power was being affected by old age. Perhaps it was his sensitivity to this that has led to his spirit playing drums instead of singing. Like all great artists, he was a perfectionist, most demanding of himself.

If you go to the Crosbyana Room at Gonzaga to admire his Oscar, gold and platinum recordings, and other memorabilia, listen very carefully. Are those faint sounds of drum rhythms in the background? If so, just relax and enjoy—you may be hearing from that most mellow fellow, Bing Crosby, in spirit.

Ogopogo's American Cousin

There are a few rumors, mere whispers really, that something strange might be lurking beneath the sparkling waters of Lake Chelan. Is there a dark secret in this beautiful lake, located on the eastern flanks of the Cascades?

A small but growing number of people believe that a monstrous creature may live in Lake Chelan, an animal comparable to Lake Okanagan's famous Ogopogo.

British Columbia's Lake Okanagan lies about ninety miles northeast of Washington's Lake Chelan. The mysterious monster Ogopogo said to live in it has become so famous that it was featured on a stamp issued by the Canadian Post Office in 1990. Ogopogo, also known by its Salish Indian name of Naitaka, or "Lake Demon," has intrigued people for more than 150 years. In 1860, two horses that were being led through the lake by a farmer, although known to be good swimmers, disappeared without a trace. In 1872, the first reported sighting of a strange, reptile-like animal was described. Canadians like to point out that Scotland's Loch Ness monster only entered modern history with a 1926 sighting, so Ogopogo is older than its Scottish counterpart.

Could Ogopogo have an American cousin dwelling in relative obscurity in Lake Chelan? Indian legends throughout the Pacific Northwest hint that odd, possibly supernatural creatures live in the region's natural, glacial lakes. The Salish tribe in British Columbia used to propitiate lake demons with sacrifices of small animals. Some stories assert that murderers were condemned by the gods to dwell evermore in lakes like Okanagan—or Chelan.

There is something about large lakes, especially very deep lakes, that fosters legends about strange monsters dwelling in them. Why are there so many stories of huge fish, enormous sea snakes, marine dinosaurs, and other fearsome monsters living in large bodies of water? One contributing factor is our fear of the unknown, our anxiety over what we cannot see readily or clearly. The depths can hide fierce predators, as the movie *Jaws* dramatized so effectively.

The best known of all lake monsters is, of course, Nessie, the elusive Loch Ness monster of Scotland. The legendary Nessie has been joined now by others. Lake Winnipeg, in Canada, supposedly hosts a monster called Winnie. The Russians claim that the world's deepest lake, Lake Baikal, is inhabited by monsters. Early explorers claimed to have encounters with gigantic water serpents in Lake Erie and Lake Michigan. Big lakes and big monsters go hand in hand.

Nessie, Ogopogo, and Lake Chelan's as yet unnamed monster have more in common than just their general appearance. Their homes are very similar. Loch Ness and Lake Chelan are very deep freshwater bodies. They occupy parts of enormous natural trenches in the earth's crust, the result of titanic forces in the crust that created parallel fractures across mountainous terrain. Loch Ness is in the Great Glen, a valley that nearly splits Scotland from east to west. Lake Chelan lies within a similar trenchlike depression on the eastern side of the Cascades. Chelan is 55 miles long and is an astonishing 1,500 feet deep. In places, its bottom is 400 feet below sea level. Who knows what secrets these depths conceal? Why isn't Lake Chelan's alleged monster as well known as its Scottish and British Columbian counterparts? Perhaps it is relative isolation. Lake Chelan's northern reaches are flanked by rugged mountains soaring 8,000 feet above the lake. Relatively few visitors have had opportunities to observe the mystery denizen of Lake Chelan.

Are Ogopogo and its presumed American cousin in Lake Chelan mere figments of overactive imaginations? There are no clear, authenticated photos of these creatures, at least pictures that could not have been faked, or which might just show ripples in the water from boat wakes. Serious scientific expeditions have failed to prove that the supposed monsters really exist. On the other hand, there is no proof that such creatures could not be lurking in the depths.

Marine biologists say that the questions is not, "Is there a monster?" The proper question is, "Could there be a monster?" It comes down to food. A breeding population of large carnivores would require a large food base of fish. Some scientists claim that, yes, there are enough fish to support large meat-eating creatures. Others point out that if Ogopogo and its kind are cold-blooded animals like dinosaurs are assumed to have been, they could, like alligators, live months between meals.

Even if Lake Chelan's alleged monster exists only in imagination, a visit to the spectacular lake will reward tourists with wonderful scenery. And, you never know, you might get a quick glimpse of an intriguing legend. Generous samples of the excellent wines produced in the southern lakeshore vineyards might enhance your chances of witnessing the monster.

Mysteries of the Sacred Cave

It can only be imagined what rituals once were held in the sacred cave in centuries past. What is certain is that the Manresa Grotto was used for religious ceremonies among the Kalispel Indians long before the arrival of white explorers and missionaries.

This cavern, above the east bank of the Pend Oreille River in the northeast corner of the Evergreen State, seems to have been utilized both for group worship and solitary prayer. A space within the cave complex, referred to now as the "auditorium," contained a stone altar and flat stones for seating. This 60-foot-wide and 25-five-foot-deep chamber is not the only space underground in the interrelated cavities that has religious significance to the Kalispels. Rumors persist that other rooms, never revealed to nontribal members, contain rock drawings. These petroglyphs allegedly symbolically show the past and the future of the Kalispels. These symbols only reveal their messages to those shamans who have learned the ancient ways of their people. Supposedly, some truths about future catastrophes are not shared with others because of their terrible meaning.

Some speculate that coming-of-age ceremonies were held at the stone altar before Christian contact. A group of elders would lead the young man or woman into the sacred cave, explaining that the cavern represented the hospitality and support given to humans from the earth itself. Symbolically, they were in the womb of the earth, readying themselves to be reborn as full members of their tribe, equipped with all the knowledge that was their birthright. The initiate then would be left alone in the cave, with only water and a supply of fuel for the sacred fire that burned in a stone bowl. This fire must not go out during the three days the initiate would spend in solitary prayer and contemplation of the mysteries of life and death. Small bundles of dried leaves were to be added to the fire to encourage dreams. These dreams would, in fact, be direct communication with the spirits of nature—earth, water, sky, and fire. It is probable that these dream-induced materials included plants with hallucinogenic properties.

When the tribal elders reentered the cave to complete the ceremony, they brought in small animals to be sacrificed. The stone bowl that had contained the sacred fire now was filled with fresh blood from the sacrifices. Some believe that this blood was then ritually consumed by all present, ensuring long life and good hunting.

When a missionary priest, Father Desmet, arrived in the early nineteenth century, he quickly realized that the sacred cave's role in Kalispel culture and tradition was so prominent that he could not ignore it. He had a sudden inspiration, a revelation. St. Ignatius, by tradition, had retreated to a cave in Spain in order to focus on his prayers. The cave, still the site of pilgrimages today, was named Manresa Grotto. Father Desmet renamed the Kalispels' sacred cave Manresa and began holding Mass in the cavern before the newly consecrated stone altar. By his action, the sacred cave was still a sacred cave, but in a different context. It is still used for Mass every year at Easter.

No one knows, or at least acknowledges, whether other, pre-Christian ceremonies might be held in other underground spaces there. Are the sacred rock drawings still intact and still offering glimpses of both the past and future?

The Noisy Ghosts of Ruby

Don't bother looking for Ruby. It isn't there anymore and hasn't been for more than a century and a quarter. Even the foundation stones of its buildings are scattered apart, giving only professional archeologists any clue as to the location of the long-gone town that once was the county seat of Okanogan County. Ruby once was a quite a place. It was known as the "Babylon of Washington Territory," and that title was not meant to be complimentary, at least among God-fearing, law-abiding folk.

There is very little to see at Ruby, and that includes ghosts. A few people claim to have seen spirits at Ruby, but they also admit to having consumed spirits of another kind. Many more people, with or without the assistance of alcoholic beverages, have heard things at or near Ruby that they shouldn't have heard out in the forlorn wilderness. The location lies off an unmarked dirt road that runs north of Conconully in the Salmon Meadows section of Okanogan National Forest.

Are the strange sounds near Ruby the auditory phantoms of the town's raucous life in the 1880s, or are they just illusions associated with the strong winds of the area? No one can be sure. Gunfire is commonly heard, or so some believe, accompanied by sounds of drunken merriment and honky-tonk saloon music. It is said that the sound of a judge's gavel can be discerned just before the phantom sounds fade away. Did a faint voice or voices shout "Free Butch!" or was that just the wind? Some believe that the reference to Butch may originate in a reliving of a famous trial in Ruby's short but lively existence.

Historians agree that peace and dignity were not hallmarks of early Ruby. Its citizens were miners hoping to share in the gold strikes in the rich Salmon Creek district. These miners drank a lot of homemade corn whiskey, known locally as "crackskull," a reference to the ferocious hangovers it caused. Taking on a load of crackskull made for a riotous evening, followed by a notably cranky morning for these heavily armed and reckless young men. As they said, it was a lively and noisy town.

The local butcher, known simply as Butch, was very popular, for two reasons: His meat was good and cheap and he generally bought rounds for everyone in the Bucket of Blood, the town's most elegant saloon. Butch was a notorious cattle rustler, which explained his cheap meat.

The story is that a band of irate cattlemen descended on Ruby looking for Butch. They thoughtfully brought a stout rope with them. They found Butch in the Bucket of Blood. Butch's many friends, recent beneficiaries of his generosity, rallied to his defense. It was a standoff, or possibly, the start of a civil war. The sheriff decided that Butch's trial should be held in Colville. Butch and two guards headed out of town. Butch, generous as always, shared a jug of crackskull with his guards, who then fell asleep. Butch wandered off, then fell into a drunken stupor himself. All three were easily found by the posse sent out after them. Maybe it was the loud snoring.

The trial was held in Ruby, conveniently in the saloon. Butch bought the first round of drinks. And the second and third. The judge bought the fourth round after declaring a mistrial on account of the entire jury's passing out. That trial was so popular that it was reenacted every Saturday night for months. It seems as though the ghostly echoes of the event are with us still, blowing in the wind. Listen carefully when in Ruby. It might help to drink up first.

Couriers of Souls

This incident happened more than twenty years ago in the city of Wenatchee. It was related on the grounds of anonymity, so we'll call the reporter Jack. Jack believes that his experience is just one example of a seldom observed but actually routine event. Jack believes that he really saw a soul being transported to the next world, and that this supernatural courier was an owl. Interestingly, this image of a bird carrying a soul on its final journey is one that transcends space and time. Many cultures around the world, ancient and contemporary, share similar traditions.

Jack had agreed to stay at the house of a dying friend for an evening to help a private nurse care for the patient. The nurse was nervous about being in the isolated house on the edge of town, so Jack agreed to keep her company.

A recent college graduate, Jack was in his first year of teaching. One of his former teachers, a longtime friend, was now a school principal and had hired Jack to teach in the same school from which he had graduated. Sadly, the principal now lay dying of bone cancer and had decided to spend his last days at home rather than in an institution surrounded by machines.

Jack and the nurse were chatting quietly in the kitchen when the man's two dogs began an unearthly howling out in the backyard. Concerned that they might have gotten into trouble somehow, Jack rushed outside to find them. The two dogs were cowered beneath their master's bedroom window—crying their hearts out in mourning, Jack immediately sensed. As Jack watched in awe tinged with fear, an owl appeared to fly out of the bedroom window, though the window itself was closed. The bird seemed to hover effortlessly for a long time. Then, as though filmed in slow motion, it flapped its wings and climbed steadily into the darkening sky of dusk. In a moment, it was out of sight.

Thoroughly shaken by what seemed to be a supernatural vision, Jack staggered back into the house. He and the nurse rushed to his friend's room, where they discovered that he had just breathed his last breath. To this day, Jack is convinced that he witnessed his friend's soul being borne up to heaven by a mystical bird.

In folk traditions around the world, some animals are thought to play roles in supernatural events, either as ghostly beings or as living creatures sensitized to the spirit world. Cats especially are said to be witches' "familiars" or henchmen, and black dogs frequently warn of death approaching. Birds often fill the role of carrying the deceased's spirit on to the next world. But why birds?

People always have admired and envied birds for their ability to fly and soar upwards to the heavens, unhindered by earthly bounds. It is why angels are perceived as having wings. As a student of anthropology, Jack knew that birds feature prominently in death traditions around the world. Birds often were, and are, seen as omens of death, the very souls of the dead, or carriers of souls. The ancient Egyptians, for example, portrayed human souls as birds with human heads, and the souls of the pharaohs were pictured as hawks. The Aztecs thought that the dead were reborn as birds. Some African tribes sacrificed a bird and placed it on a corpse in order that the bird's spirit would transport the person's spirit to the next world. In Irish folklore, seagulls embody the souls of drowning victims. Birds with dark plumage, crows and ravens, and nocturnal birds like owls, are believed to be harbingers of death. Are they also couriers of souls to the spirit world? Jack would say yes.

The Bed of Death

The bed of death is not a bed at all. And it is not a deathbed, because no one has actually died on it. The bed of death, nonetheless, has earned its grim name and notorious reputation. It is actually a tombstone, a flat, horizontal marker rather than the much more common vertical stones. The cemetery in which it is located will not be identified. The tombstone has been associated with so many deaths that some have come to regard the stone itself as inherently evil. There have already been several attempts to deface the alleged bed of death. In addition, the cemetery's operators do not wish to encourage the kind of macabre tourism that the grave has attracted. Suffice it to say that the bed of death is found in a cemetery in metropolitan Spokane.

The legend of the bed of death begins with a tragedy, fittingly enough. A beautiful teenage girl had committed suicide. A perfect storm of negative events led to the deep depression that induced her to take a massive overdose of potent sleeping pills. Formerly an honor student, her grades had plummeted in all but one subject. Rumors spread that she had an intense love affair with a married teacher. She had neglected all her other courses, which contributed to a rejection of all her college applications. The suspected lover had abruptly ended their relationship. A beloved grandparent died suddenly and her pet dog was killed on a highway.

The girl's distraught parents soon learned that their church would not permit a person who committed suicide to be buried in the affiliated cemetery. As the parents searched for an appropriate resting place for their daughter, a psychic gave them unsolicited advice that they should be bury her beneath a full-length, heavy horizontal stone to keep her tormented soul from rising from her grave and wandering among the living. This advice was followed.

The legend is that soon after the tombstone was installed, a group of the girl's school friends visited her grave. They were motivated by sincere grief, tempered with a bit of morbid curiosity. The deceased's best friend impulsively decided to lie down atop the horizontal gravestone. She wanted, she said, to communicate with her friend's spirit. Within a week, she was dead, having choked to death on a piece of steak. That following Halloween night, two young men, having just downed a six-pack of beer each, decided to commune with the dead by taking turns lying on the tombstone. They met their grisly deaths in a horrific auto accident soon afterward. Was it just another alcohol-fueled accident or something more sinister?

Now labeled the bed of death, the reputation of the evil tombstone spread quickly. A local college fraternity decided to challenge its new pledges to lie down on the notorious bed and be photographed there to prove their bravery. One of these brave men was electrocuted in a freak accident at the fraternity house. The other, a trained lifeguard, was drowned while trying to rescue a toddler who fell into a lake.

As the death toll mounted, it became a nasty prank to lure an unsuspecting person to the gravesite and "accidentally" knock them prone on the bed of death. It is not known how many deaths may have resulted from this. Be careful not to trip over any flat tombstones. You just never know.

Death Notice

This family tradition was related on the grounds of anonymity by a family now living in the Spokane area. We'll call them the Johnsons. The event itself happened in the early 1960s. Those directly involved have now passed on, leaving behind an interesting, if a bit unsettling, story.

Over the years, there have been many similar stories of people believing supernatural communications of some kind regarding the death of a loved one. It is most common concerning the death of a child, sibling, or spouse. A vivid dream, a sudden phenomenon, or some such awareness will reach the recipient hours, sometimes days, before the actual phone call, letter, or telegram. Often, the recently dead reach out to reassure their loved one of their transition to a happier world, a new spiritual existence. This paranormal contact usually has a calming effect on the survivor. Is it possible that the deceased's spirit, newly freed from its earthly bonds, can somehow reach across space in an instant? Many believe so, including the Johnsons.

The family's greatest joy was the recent arrival of a grandson, their first grandchild. Unfortunately, from the grandparents' perspective, they could not personally witness all the "firsts"—words, steps, and so on—because the baby's father was in the early stages of his chosen career with the State Department. An aspiring diplomat, he had recently been assigned to the embassy in newly independent Uganda in east Africa. Plum posts like London or Paris came at the end of a successful career, not at the beginning.

About six months after the younger Johnson's departure for Uganda, the new grandmother had a most disturbing dream, or was it just a dream? It must have been around three in the morning. She was suddenly aware of a tall, glowing female figure in her room, standing near the window. The figure, whose back was to her, appeared to be dressed in a long white robe with a hood over her head. Soundlessly, the apparition turned toward her. Cradled in its arms was the still, silent figure of her tiny grandson. He was wrapped in a distinctive red, white, and blue hand-knitted blanket his grandmother had made for him. The hooded figure, its face hidden in shadow, appeared to gently rock the little baby in her arms, then slowly faded away.

The long-distance phone call came two hours later. Her son tearfully told of the infant's death. Tragically, he had been stricken by a very high fever of unknown origin. The usual technique of placing him in an ice-filled bath could not be done. Power outages had melted any ice that might have been available. Recent civil unrest meant no antibiotics could be found. "He's with the angels now," said her son, not realizing how true that was. Mrs. Johnson always believed that an angel had brought the baby's spirit to her at the moment of death, for her blessing and acceptance.

Ghost Town

There were a lot of little towns like Govan, ghost towns whose purpose had slowly faded away, towns abandoned as a result of too few customers for what they had to offer. Likely there are other places that are ghost towns in the other sense of the word—towns full of ghosts.

Govan is, or more exactly, used to be on Route 2, between Wilbur and Almira, south of the Grand Coulee Dam. Typical of such small towns in the dry country east of the Cascades, Govan existed as a center of economic and social life for the surrounding ranches and farms. Govan was born in the late nineteenth century and died a slow death in the 1930s. The town's decay wasn't the fault of those who lived and worked there. Govan's citizens were bright enough and hardworking enough. It was a combination of forces beyond their control that doomed the town, which might explain the looks of forlorn puzzlement that characterize Govan's ghosts to this day.

In its heyday, Govan was like a neighborhood shopping center in a city. It supplied the daily wants of the people in the surrounding area. It had grocery, hardware, clothing, and farm supply stores. It had a post office, a school, and a church. The automobile age brought a service station, along with the seeds of doom.

Just as is true today, most folks aren't willing to travel far in order to buy everyday necessities like fresh food, postage stamps, gasoline, soap, or the like. For that kind of purchase, the closer the better, which in the days of horse-drawn wagons and unpaved roads, was within a few miles. Cars and paved roads changed the rules by letting people travel much greater distances in the time they were willing to spend going shopping for basic needs. Why not go further for more variety of choice and more competitive prices? People could and did. School buses eliminated tiny one-room schools. Mechanization led to larger but fewer farms in the neighborhood and fewer customers for local stores.

And so Govan, and many others town like it, withered away like a houseplant that was no longer watered. The cemetery remained, of course, but it was no longer tended; tall weeds obscured the headstones.

Today, only two buildings remain: the former post office and the long-abandoned school. Some scattered foundations mark the sites of vanished houses. It is a lonely, desolate place of disappointed hopes and shattered dreams. Even the wind seems to moan as it passes by.

A couple of tourists had an interesting experience as they stopped to photograph the lonesome-looking school and post office. A middle-aged man dressed in faded, dusty farmer's overalls approached them. Would it be possible, he asked politely, to hitch a ride with them to the next town? "I've got to get out of Govan," he explained. "The town's just drying up." He looked so sad and forlorn that the couple agreed. The man climbed into the backseat. As they rode along, he related the story of Govan. "Used to be an up-and-coming place. Then the drought hit and a lot of folks moved away. Couldn't make a living, they said. No matter how hard they worked or how much they cut prices, the stores closed, one by one."

"Finally," he said, his voice just a whisper, "I had to leave too, but no one was left to bury me." At that, the couple turned toward the backseat only to see a small pile of dust on the upholstery. They had given a ride to a ghost.

Another family traveling through was intrigued by the old school, still standing though windowless and doorless. They swear they came across a classroom filled not with children, but by sad-faced adults, sitting in stunned resignation as they stared at the chalkboard and its soul-wrenching agenda for a town meeting. The meeting focused on bankruptcy. The town was bankrupt because no one could pay taxes on foreclosed properties. The mayor had committed suicide when his store failed and his family left him. The townspeople's dreams were over. They had been defeated by economic forces beyond their control. As the tourists watched in fascinated horror, the forms of the townspeople simply faded away, leaving only gray dust in their place. Govan really is more than a ghost town—it's a town full of ghosts.

The Picture of Determination

As her older relatives used to remark, Aunt Ellen was the "picture of determination." Her long-suffering husband, Uncle Fred, could have testified that she usually got her way. In fact, Ellen would make things so miserable for anyone who crossed her that she had trained her relatives and friends to give in quickly to her requests and suggestions. Resistance was futile. Patient argument and stacks of facts made no impression on Aunt Ellen. There was her way and there was the wrong way. Not that she was unloved. Often, she turned out to be absolutely right, and she could be a very kind and generous person, but she surely was determined to get her way.

Uncle Fred and Aunt Ellen had made a tidy sum with their large apple orchard near Wenatchee. As they used to joke, "Money does grow on trees!" Prudently invested, their money grew in real estate and the stock market. Fred and Ellen never had children, but their fertile siblings produced a dozen nieces and nephews, all of whom dreamed of inheritance. Fred died first. At the luncheon following his burial, Aunt Ellen announced that after her own death, each of her nieces and nephews would inherit a modest sum and each would, in turn, occupy her house for one month. During that month, she said, her spirit would come to them, if they were properly receptive, and direct them to the bulk of her fortune, which she had converted into gold coins. "I've two suggestions," she told her stunned audience, suddenly very attentive. "Don't change anything, and try to see things my way." Even after her eventual death it appeared her way would be the right way. "My spirit will be watching you when you are staying in my house," she promised, revealing a hitherto unsuspected interest in spiritualism.

After Ellen's death, one nephew after another moved into her house for their one month's occupancy and treasure hunt. The first to try, Michael, was not attuned at all to communication with this deceased aunt. He searched diligently through the house and even dug up some flower beds, to no avail. The second heir, Bryce, went so far as to hire a medium to conduct a séance in Ellen's house. It was not successful, and the medium blamed Bryce's openly hostile attitude for the failure to contact Ellen.

Then it was Laura's turn. She had been a favorite of her Aunt Ellen, because she was able to see beyond Ellen's peremptory insistence on doing things her way to the sound and good intentions and reasoning behind it. Laura decided to focus on communing with Ellen's spirit by meditation. "Don't change anything," Ellen had admonished, so Laura restored a portrait of Ellen that had hung on a wall opposite a window looking out to the backyard. Ellen herself had often sat looking out that window at the sole survivor of her original apple orchard, now mostly uprooted and sold off as house lots. Ellen had insisted on preserving that old apple tree, long past bearing age, as it reminded her of the days when she and Fred had planted their first orchard, the foundation of her wealth. Now, Ellen's portrait looked out at the view she had treasured in life.

That evening while Laura was sound asleep, she dreamed of a visit from Ellen's ghost. "Laura, try to see things the way I saw them," was the rather cryptic message. "See things the way Aunt Ellen saw them," Laura repeated to herself. Suddenly inspired, she stood in front of Ellen's portrait and looked out the window. There in the center of her view was the gnarled old apple tree. On impulse, Laura took a spade and began digging at the base of the old tree. Soon she came across several quart mason jars filled with gold coins. Ellen's spirit had pointed her towards the bulk of her fortune, just as she had promised. Ellen, true to form, had determined to give her money to the relative who was most attuned to her wishes.

"Walk, Don't Run"

The school is haunted. As far as most of the kids go, there is no doubt about this. The current staff members are a little more reserved about expressing their opinions, though they tend to look over their shoulders when discussing the haunting. Not that the haunting is a bad thing; the alleged spirit definitely is on the side of law and order. It's just that having a phantom teacher in and about the building can be a tad unnerving.

As there is no sense in unduly alarming those who may never have any contact with this spirit, the school shall remain unnamed. Suffice it to say that it is a brown brick, two-story structure set next to a wide avenue heading north from downtown Spokane. It is named for a relatively undistinguished president who happened to be in office when the school was built.

Ghosts don't wear nametags, so the identity of this one is not certain; however, some old-timers, whose grandchildren now attend their old school, believe they know whose spirit lingers in the halls. This phantom's behavior precisely matches that of Miss Alice Greenwood, a longtime fixture at the school. Miss Greenwood is thought to have started her career there when the school opened. She remained at her post for forty years. Many have reason to believe that she is still on duty, or rather her ghost is.

To say that Miss Greenwood was a disciplinarian is like commenting that Marine drill sergeants can be strict. There was something about Miss Greenwood that commanded obedience and cooperation. She expected it. Her tongue-lashings, delivered in a soft voice and without resort to abusive language, were so effective because even the most recalcitrant pupils recognized her sincerity and determination, backed by a sound slap on the bottom as necessary. These slaps hurt the pride of the miscreants more than their bottoms, as Miss Greenwood doubtless intended. At the time, no one questioned her mild physical punishment techniques.

Few have actually seen Miss Greenwood's ghost, but many claim to have heard her. Apparently, she still patrols the halls, sternly correcting sloppy discipline among yet another generation. "Stay in line! No talking! Do not touch one another!" The sharp commands are most likely to be heard during periodic fire drills, which the once-living teacher took very seriously. Horseplay during drills was not tolerated; slaps on the behind followed any inattention to her commands.

Legend has it that, years after Miss Greenwood had gone to that great homeroom in the sky, an overheated oil furnace had suddenly sent clouds of oily black smoke through the building. Terrorized, the children ran down the halls, pushing others to the floor when the authoritative voice of Miss Greenwood was heard. "Walk, don't run! Stay in line!" rang out, followed by a few quick swats on the seats of the undisciplined. There is little doubt that the phantom teacher's intervention prevented a panic that easily could have led to injuries or worse.

Disciplining a Spirit

The medium who recounted these events did so with the understanding that she would remain anonymous. We'll call her Liz. Mediums are those who are especially sensitive to the spirit world. They act as intermediaries between the living and the spirits of the dead. Like most mediums, Liz became aware of her special gifts in childhood. She could hear and see what adults could not sense. Commonly, parents and other adults express strong disbelief and disapproval to the youngsters reporting these phenomena, out of concern that the child might be classified as mentally ill or mocked as an unscrupulous attention-seeker. Thus, many potential mediums are discouraged from developing their special talents. Liz was particularly fortunate in that her aunt Nell, who had experienced some communications with the spirit world as a child, accepted Liz's claims as real and encouraged her to accept herself and use her mystic powers to help others.

Most cultures have traditions of mediums, whether they are called witches, wizards, seers, witch doctors, or shamans. Curiously, most mediums in Western culture are women, while most Native American shamans are men. Like many other sincere mediums, Liz has decided not to capitalize on or exploit her gifts, only accepting reimbursement for travel expenses when appropriate. Her most interesting case started with a frantic phone call from a friend of a friend, who lived in Wenatchee. She was being harassed by a poltergeist and thought that if she could communicate with this spirit, then she could persuade it to cease and desist. This intrigued Liz, whose powers usually involved the recently bereaved attempting to contact their loved ones. She went to Wenatchee.

Ten minutes after arriving at the haunted home, Liz agreed that a poltergeist, or "noisy spirit," was present. Dishes flew off tables, and small decorative items crashed onto the floors. A séance, Liz told her client, would not be appropriate considering the evidently hostile attitude of the spirit. Liz requested that she be left alone in the house so that she could attempt a communication.

Liz did succeed in establishing contact, unfortunately with a strongly negative spirit. The poltergeist introduced himself by tossing books out of the bookcase onto the floor. He said his name was Jack and defiantly admitted to causing chaos in the house for no apparent reason other than the unfortunate woman's resemblance to a teacher he once had, a Miss Virginia Field. Liz questioned him after he calmed down. It seems this was the phantom of a nine-year-old boy who was killed in traffic while crossing a street. His spirit had no home to return to, as the parents who nearly ignored him in life had moved far away after his untimely death. The only adult who had paid attention to him was Miss Field, who was a strict disciplinarian. While he resented the attempts to discipline him, he did respect her for "taking the time to bring out the best in him," as she said.

Liz tried to persuade him to leave the family in peace, but was answered only by another shower of books, followed by a few potted plants crashing to the floor. His strongly negative energies caused her to withdraw from the confrontation, a rare defeat for her.

Then Liz had an inspiration. She checked with a local school district. Virginia Field had died of heart failure about six months after the tragic accident that killed one of her students, Jack O'Brien. Liz put herself into a meditating trance and called up the spirit of Virginia Field. Liz persuaded Miss Field's ghost to reach out to Jack, which she was quite willing to do. "Jack could be a handful," replied the teacher's spirit, "but he was not fundamentally bad, just acting out his frustrations with a loveless home life. I'll talk with him."

Sure enough, Jack the poltergeist never returned to harass anyone. Sometimes it takes a spirit to discipline a spirit.

Ending a Haunting

In the movies, haunted houses are either Gothic monstrosities or decaying Victorian mansions, not new suburban houses. Age and quaintness seem to be necessary ingredients in ghost stories, but one family learned differently, and they learned the hard way. The family, whom we'll call the Petersons, was excited about their new home. It was a great buy. Even the town's name, Opportunity, was optimistic.

The house was only four years old, one of a whole subdivision of so-called "McMansions," popular in the first years of the new century. It had a two-story entrance hall, four bedrooms, two-and-a-half baths, and a kitchen "to die for," so the real estate agent said. She neglected to mention that someone had died for it, or at least in it. Suicides are so depressing, and why spoil a sale?

As so often seems to be the case, no one noticed anything unusual, at least for a few weeks after moving in. The ghost seemed to give them a kind of stress-free honeymoon before making its presence known. And, also a common theme in haunted house stories, the dog was the first to sense something wrong in the supernatural sense.

Rudy, the family's five-year-old Bouvier, didn't look very bright. Maybe it was the way that his curly black hair hung down over his eyes, or the way he never learned that he couldn't catch squirrels who'd already run up a tree. He had other, endearing qualities, like a fierce determination to protect his human family from any threats. As the oldest child observed, Rudy might be a little goofy, but he was very brave. As it turned out, he needed to be brave.

Rudy's official, assigned bed was in an alcove in the kitchen, but he liked to visit the kids, or even the parents, in their upstairs bedrooms when invited. He quickly learned that, on going up the stairs to the second floor, if all bedroom doors were closed, he should go back down to his own bed. An open bedroom door was an invitation to come in for the night. Whining and scratching at doors had no effect on exclusion decisions, and Rudy came to accept that.

One memorable night, Rudy uncharacteristically alarmed everyone with spasms of loud barks, followed by frantically running up the stairs and hurling himself against the door of the master bedroom. When the door was finally opened, an obviously agitated Rudy started back down the stairs, looking over his shoulder and pausing as if to say, "Come on, follow me, something weird is going on!" Rudy was followed into the kitchen, where he crouched in front of the rocking chair, giving his trademark menacing, deep-throated growl. The rocking chair was rocking by itself, without any visible occupant. The rocking grew violent, and the chair tipped over on its side. No one, including Rudy, got back to sleep that night.

The following nights saw a repetition of this unsettling event, or sometimes unexplained footsteps in the kitchen late at night. Each episode ended in Rudy's barking and howling.

Convinced that their lovely house was infested by some supernatural force, the Petersons contacted a spiritualist who offered to spend the night in their kitchen in an effort to contact the ghost, if that was what it was. Contact was established. It seemed that the spirit was that of the previous owner, a man with a tragic end to his financial nightmare. He had bought the new house with very little down payment, lured by the assumption that values would continue to rise. But the housing market collapsed and he lost his job; his wife then left him, taking his children out of state. About to be evicted, penniless, and despondent, he sat in his kitchen one night and swallowed a whole bottle of sleeping pills washed down with a liter of scotch.

Now, his spirit seemed trapped in the house. Could the Petersons help his spirit move on to the next world by praying for his soul? They asked the spiritualist. The family agreed to include him in their daily devotions, and peace followed. Rudy, and the power of prayer, had triumphed. Rudy basks in the admiration of his human family, although he still can't catch squirrels.

Southeast
Washington

WASHINGTON'S SOUTHEASTERN REGION IS BOUNDED ON THE SOUTH AND east by the state's boundaries with Oregon and Idaho. To the west lie the mighty Cascades and the northern boundary runs along a line from Ellensburg to Moses Lake to Cheney. Important towns include Yakima, Richland, Kennewick, and Walla Walla.

As in all regions, history is reflected in many of the stories of the supernatural. The gruesome ghosts of an infamous massacre of missionaries haunt the site of their mission. A crudely built pioneer train still rumbles down ghost tracks and a boisterous dog learns not to follow a UFO. A nuclear engineer decides to come back from the dead as a dog, and a judge and jury continually relive a famous trial featuring free-flowing whiskey. The spirit of a distinguished, if controversial, Supreme Court justice is said to haunt the replica of his office. In another tale of southeastern Washington, the ancient petroglyphs, or rock carvings and paintings, on the Columbia River are alleged to communicate warnings of future events.

Shades of the Rawhide Railroad

The old-fashioned steam locomotive, with its flaring smokestack and kerosene headlamp, seems to wobble along the tracks, rocking alarmingly from side to side. The speed is little more than that of a brisk walk. A single, crude-looking passenger car is drawn along behind the locomotive, followed by a string of flat cars loaded with large wooden barrels. Oddly, a collie dog is seen running along the tracks, barking frantically at cattle strolling along the right-of-way.

As the observers turn their attention from the collie back to the train, the train seems to evaporate before their eyes. All that remains is the mournful echo of the steam whistle. On closer inspection, the embankment along which the train appeared is empty—no train, no tracks. The whole vision was just a mirage, a ghost train. The long-vanished Rawhide Railroad has just made another of its supernatural visits to the land of the living.

If, as many believe, ghostly apparitions are a form of energy imprinted in the environment by people and events of the past, the Rawhide Railroad is an echo of a single pioneer's vision and entrepreneurial spirit. Few people combine an extraordinary vision of the future with the sustained drive to make it into reality. D. S. Baker, a medical doctor by training, was such a man. He was quick to perceive that Walla Walla had a bright future as a wheat milling and shipment point, if only a railroad connected it with the Columbia River's steamboats. Walla Walla already was an important supply center for the burgeoning mining country in nearby northern Idaho. The owners of fertile wheatlands of the neighborhood found that shipments to the Pacific ports were handicapped by the high rates charged by wagons operating over poor roads. Baker decided that a railroad to the little river port of Wallula was a golden opportunity.

This bold vision attracted only ridicule. Baker used all his savings to order a locomotive from Pittsburgh and have it sent by ship all the way around Cape Horn to Portland, and then up the Columbia River by riverboat. It took him three years, from 1872 to 1875, to build a 28-mile railroad from Wallula to Walla Walla. He would pay for a mile or two of track as he earned money from delivering babies and setting broken limbs. Baker called it the Walla Walla and Columbia. His amused neighbors called it the Rawhide Railroad, because it was so crudely homemade. The lone passenger car was built by local blacksmiths and carpenters; it was christened "the Hearse" by doubtful locals, because the rickety car often fell off the tracks. The hearse didn't attract many customers, but the Rawhide line was a success at carrying barrels of flour to Wallula and the world beyond. Dr. Baker cleared a profit of more than

$68,000 in one shipment of wheat from Walla Walla to England. People stopped laughing and the collie Bob got a full-time job clearing the tracks of cattle before the Rawhide Railroad rambled down the tracks at 15 miles an hour. Baker's was a powerful dream fulfilled, and his vision still steams down the tracks in ghostly form. Should you spot the phantom of the old Rawhide, just wave; it can't run you down, and it is an amazing reminder of Washington's colorful past when wild dreams sometimes came true.

Hog's Unfortunate Ordeal

It was all Hog's fault, really. He wandered away once too often, that's all. Hog was handsome and friendly, but not very bright. He was an Irish setter, originally named Mahogany after his lustrous, reddish coat. The children in the family couldn't pronounce his full name; they called him Hog, and that name stuck. Hog's eagerness to consume dog food, people food, small plush animals, and rubber bones made his new name appropriate.

It became evident early that Hog would never be the valedictorian of his pet obedience class. When he needed to go outside to do his business, he would stand by the door and bark. Approved and applauded behavior, but with one quirk. Hog would wait expectantly at the hinge side of the door, never remembering that the other side of the door would open for his relief. Lovable but not too smart was the family's consensus.

Hog's human family lived on the southwest edge of Yakima, near the airport. Yakima is famed as a fruit processing center and gateway to the Yakima Valley wine country, which boasts fifty wineries. It also has achieved fame as the site of the greatest number of UFO sightings reported per capita of any American city. Mount Rainier, to the west-northwest, is the locale of the first official UFO report in America. The vicinity of Mount Adams, to Yakima's west-southwest, is another hotbed of UFO activity. Hog's encounter fits a pattern, geographically speaking.

Hog liked to chase rabbits, squirrels, other dogs, and even scraps of paper blowing in the wind. He didn't seem to care if he caught anything; the chase itself was the thing. The time he chased the UFO, however, was the last time he would go heedlessly bounding after the enticing unknown.

The family, whom we'll call the Parsons, was having a picnic supper in their backyard. It was dusk on a warm summer night. Hog, true to his name, was begging for handouts, having already finished his own bowl. Seemingly out of nowhere, a silvery, disc-shaped object appeared. It seemed to float over their heads at about 200 feet, suspended noiselessly above.

The family went silent, dumbfounded. Hog went berserk. He began barking furiously while running in tight circles. The strange craft drifted slowly away, as though mocking the frantic dog. Hog leaped over the fence and followed the UFO down West Washington Avenue. The chase was on and Hog was now running full speed.

The Parsons piled into their car and chased after Hog and the UFO. Then, a few miles down the road, it happened. The UFO stopped abruptly. Hog was directly beneath it when a brilliant purple light pierced the gathering gloom. As the family watched from their car, the courageous, if foolhardy, dog was drawn up inside the beam of light as though on wires. He disappeared into the belly of the UFO. Within minutes, Hog reappeared and slowly descended within the shaft of light. As Hog touched down, the strange craft suddenly accelerated towards the sinking sun.

Hog stood absolutely still for a few minutes before he laid down moaning. He seemed to be in a trance. The Parsons picked him up and put him in the car and returned home. Hog was abnormally quiet for a few days. His interest in chasing anything beyond his own backyard had disappeared. Although his appetite soon returned, Hog was strangely subdued after his experience with the UFO. Any low-flying craft frightened him into hiding under the porch, proving that even Hog can learn from experience, although he still waits patiently at the hinge side of the door.

Don't Ignore a Will, or a Spirit

Uncle Fred died twice. Maybe. It depends on whether you believe that Fred's mystical prediction actually came true. Uncle Fred in the flesh, age 90, died back in 2000. Uncle Fred in spirit died five years after, or so some believe; this time he was buried in a pet cemetery.

Uncle Fred was, as they say, eccentric. The difference between eccentric and crazy often seems to come down to money. Rich folks who proclaim strange beliefs or exhibit odd behavior tend to be thought of as eccentric. Poor people with the same out-of-step attitudes might be considered mentally ill.

Fred firmly believed in life after death, but his version of immortality was his own take on this concept, one shaped by his career in nuclear energy research. Young Fred arrived in Richland in 1943, one of thousands of newcomers brought in to work on a top-secret government project—the Manhattan Project. The tiny village of 247 people in 1942 quickly became a town of 16,000 two years later. The almost-empty sage plains north of town had become the Atomic City, as it was known. The remote desert along the Columbia River's Hanford Reach, where the great river briefly flows north and east, became the Hanford Atomic Site.

Nuclear fission was an awesome mystery in the beginning. Radiation's effects were unknown but feared. Workers at the Hanford Site repeatedly were reminded about conscientiously following safety precautions. Fred somehow became convinced that his work with radioactive materials over the years, even though he never was exposed to dangerous levels, could energize his spirit, as he put it. He concluded that his spirit would migrate into another body when he died. Furthermore, he asserted, he could choose his next form of existence. It couldn't be in another human body, which was occupied already by its own immortal soul. Fred fixated on the idea that his spirit could, and would, enter the body of his pet. Accordingly, Fred kept a succession of large, handsome dogs. As one died of old age, it would be replaced by a new puppy, destined to receive Fred's spirit if it outlived his master, Fred believed. Each new dog was given the same name as its predecessor, Junior. Junior always was an Alsatian, or German shepherd, a breed he admired for its intelligence, courage, and loyalty.

Fred decided to ensure that his spirit's physical being was guaranteed a long, protected, and pampered life. Childless, he chose a nephew as his heir and Junior's guardian. Shrewd investments produced a sizeable inheritance, with some unique restrictions. The nephew received a handsome monthly stipend as long as Junior was alive. Junior was to be bred and a strong male puppy kept as a kind of spirit-residence in waiting. As long as the nephew lived, Junior's bloodline would be preserved and kept in pampered comfort.

The nephew agreed to all of this, comforted and reassured by the thoughts of Uncle Fred's money. In the fullness of time, Fred's spirit undoubtedly departed his own body, which was duly buried. Junior's new master took very good care of the "dog who laid golden eggs," as he put it. But he did not give Junior the opportunity to become a father. That, the nephew decided, was totally unnecessary. When Junior died, he would simply buy an Alsatian puppy and name him Junior. Who would know?

As it turned out, it seems that Fred's spirit would know. When the nephew brought home his newly purchased purebred Junior substitute, the puppy bounded in with enthusiasm, which was short-lived. Suddenly, the pup froze in its tracks, yelped as though in pain, and ran from the house as though pursued by the Devil himself. The would-be Junior refused to enter the house again and bit the nephew on the face when he tried to drag him in. The executor of Fred's will, discovering that the nephew did not have a dog living with him, terminated the monthly payments, and as the will directed, he gave the residue of the estate to the SPCA.

It is said that the nephew was driven mad by horrific nightmares of being attacked by vicious dogs. He later committed suicide. Some believe that a phantom German shepherd makes regular visits to the grave, marking its territory with such torrents of urine that nothing grows atop that grave, not even weeds.

Order in the Court

The ghosts are heard more frequently than they are seen. Rap, rap, rap, sounds an unseen gavel. "Order in the bar, I mean, order in the court!" The gavel is pounded again and again, always in groups of three raps, each series louder than the last. Finally, the accompanying background noises of drunken laughter and conversation fade away into silence. "How finds the jury?" asks a slurred but still authoritative voice. "Innocent and generous" is the reply. "Most generous!" A piano is played with more enthusiasm than style, and the sounds of drunken merriment rise to a crescendo before dying away.

These phantom sounds, which not everyone can hear, are a ghostly reenactment of a famous incident early in Ellensburg's history. The trial of Pat Lynch was one of the highlights of the town's rowdy history as a gold-mining and ranching center.

Actually, the Ellensburg area has led a remarkable series of very different lives in its checkered history, from peaceable hunting grounds to frontier trading post to farming center to university town. The fertile Kittitas Valley provided such good hunting that the mutually hostile Wenatchee, Nez Perce, and Yakima Indians made it a neutral area, where they all could hunt in peace. This was an open land, sort of like Las Vegas once was open to all organized crime families rather than anyone's exclusive territory.

A log trading post, known as Robber's Roost, was built in 1867. The post became the nucleus of the town, eventually renamed Ellen's Burg after the wife of an early settler.

In 1870, Pat Lynch, an Irishman noted for his fiery temper, marksmanship, sense of humor, and capacity for strong drink, was on his way to Robber's Roost. He took a shortcut across land belonging to a longtime enemy. Ordered off the man's property, Pat drew down on him and killed him, then continued to Robber's Roost. Friends of the recently deceased raised a fuss, even after Pat offered to stand them a round of drinks.

Court was called into session in the saloon, the only building large enough to hold a crowd. Pat thoughtfully bought each juror, the judge, and the sheriff a bottle of whiskey. "Make it the good stuff, mind you," he told the bartender. "Not that one-week-old rotgut."

When the judge at last polled the jury, the four jurors who were still conscious agreed on a not-guilty verdict. Pat not only bought everyone present drinks, but agreed to pay for his victim's coffin as well—a generous gesture that earned him much goodwill.

It is said that Pat's trial was thereafter celebrated by nightly reenactments in the saloon that he opened in the growing town. Allegedly, the phantoms of Robber's Roost still hold a ghostly reenactment whenever they are thirsty, which is often.

The Spirit of Wild Bill

It was the eyes that they noticed first. The piercing blue eyes seemed to stare right through them, X-raying their very souls. The figure's deeply tanned and seamed face was set off by neatly trimmed white hair. A conservatively cut tweed suit and somber tie completed the image of a distinguished jurist. The California couple touring the

Yakima Valley Museum complimented the receptionist on their way out: "That mannequin of the judge in the office replica is quite impressive—so realistic!"

"There's no mannequin in the judge's office display," she replied. Sure enough, when the visitors backtracked for another look, the figure had disappeared. The exact replica of Justice William O. Douglas's Supreme Court office was empty—except, perhaps, for his now unseen spirit.

No one familiar with the story of Douglas would be surprised to learn that his ghost has been seen in his recreated office at the museum or in other locales. His ghost is said to haunt the William O. Douglas Wilderness Area to the east of Mount Rainier, which is entirely appropriate given his intense interest in protecting the environment. Some allege that his spirit has been seen participating in various protest marches and demonstrations defending environmental concerns.

As a justice of the Supreme Court, Douglas holds several records that may never be broken. At more than thirty-six years on the bench, he was the longest-serving Supreme Court justice. He may have been the most controversial justice, too. There were four unsuccessful attempts to impeach him. While he was a hero to environmentalists and civil rights activists, he was demonized by conservatives. His Supreme Court colleagues allegedly referred to him as "Wild Bill," not necessarily as a compliment.

Wild Bill may have enjoyed his nickname, as he never shied away from controversy or even notoriety. He married four times, the last two to law students some forty years his junior. He was an activist judge, fearlessly promoting his own views on interpreting the Constitution. He advanced the then-novel concept that components of the natural environment, from individual trees to forests, valleys, and whole mountain ranges, had standing in the courts; that is, they could have their interests represented in court as though they were people or corporations. This very controversial view saved many scenic and environmentally valuable areas from development. Douglas hiked the entire Appalachian Trail from Georgia to Maine to show that he was no armchair conservationist.

Although he was born in Minnesota, Douglas grew up in Yakima, attended Whitman College in Walla Walla on a scholarship, and taught high school in Yakima before going to law school.

After teaching at Yale University's law school, Douglas was nominated to the Supreme Court by President Franklin D. Roosevelt.

Actually, Wild Bill himself came close to being President William O. Douglas. Supposedly, Roosevelt informally told aides that he wanted either Bill Douglas or Harry Truman as his vice presidential running mate in 1944. Truman was approached first and said yes, and so he became president upon Roosevelt's death less than a year later. Some believe that political aides reversed Roosevelt's priorities out of concern that Douglas was too controversial and would hurt the ticket.

Nature may never again have such a vigorous defender as William O. Douglas. His spirit marches on, or at least occasionally sits in his recreated Supreme Court office in Yakima.

The Pacifist's Angels

Sunrise at Stonehenge on the summer solstice is marked by the first rays of the sun illuminating the altar stone, exactly as planned, for the great monument is, among other things, an astronomical calendar. What is surprising about this Stonehenge is that it is on the banks of the Columbia River, not England's Salisbury Plain, and it is less than a century old, not four thousand years old like the original.

The concrete replica of Stonehenge near Maryhill was begun in 1918 and completed in 1929. It is the first major memorial built to honor America's dead warriors in World War I and was the pet project of Samuel Hill, a noted lawyer and ardent pacifist. Like England's ancient monument, Washington's Stonehenge is alleged to attract the spirits of the dead, or angels, to the site. This spiritual function may well have been one reason why Sam Hill wanted to replicate Stonehenge.

Many great people are motivated by a strong compulsion. In Sam Hill's case, the compulsion was to help end wars. He was a Quaker and a pacifist, a visionary who worked toward a world of universal peace. He put his money where his heart lay, designing and financing the Peace Arch at Blaine on the Canadian border, as well as his own version of Stonehenge. But why Stonehenge?

A psychic who believes she has channeled Sam Hill's spirit has a possible answer. Hill may have been influenced by two factors:

Stonehenge's ancient reputation as a spiritual vortex and the World War I phenomena known as the Angels of Mons.

Angels are important figures in many different cultures and traditions. These supernatural beings exist in both Judeo-Christian and Islamic mythologies and are usually depicted as being messengers from God, providing divine counsel to humans and protecting individuals or sites from evil. Many people believe that everyone has a guardian angel and many deathbed visions have angels appearing as the souls of deceased relatives sent to guide the dying into paradise.

In the early days of World War I, apparitions of angels are said to have intervened in heavy fighting near the Belgian town of Mons. A combined force of British and French soldiers attacked the Germans. A fierce artillery bombardment by the Germans killed more than fifteen thousand troops in a few hours, forcing a retreat under heavy fire. Reports of phantom fighters intervening to rescue British and French wounded began to circulate. It was said that these phantoms, dressed in medieval costumes, were the spirits of the dead from the fifteenth-century battle of Agincourt, fought nearby. French soldiers saw either the archangel Michael or Joan of Arc leading the angels, while British soldiers saw visions of their legendary hero and national patron Saint George.

Hill may have wished to provide a spiritual home to the angels or phantoms of those slain in war, a place where they might enter into the subconscious of the living and convince them of the folly and waste of war.

Many believe that the original Stonehenge is a spiritual vortex, a place where psychic energies merge and intensify. Hill may have hoped that his reproduction of Stonehenge would similarly serve as a kind of spiritual magnet for angels, for the souls of those killed in wars.

People who have visited Maryhill's Stonehenge, especially near dawn or dusk, have reportedly entered brief trances in which they sensed communion with angels. A few claim to have seen angels gliding about the monument.

Lost Symbols

A few, but only a precious few, of the petroglyphs survive. These rock symbols, or pictures, are fascinating relics that can be seen on display at Columbia Hills State Park near Dallesport. The overwhelming majority of the petroglyphs carved or painted on the steep rock walls of this narrow gorge of the Columbia River are lost to history, submerged under the waters impounded by the great Dalles Dam, which was completed in 1956. The Dalles is a place where the mighty Columbia River cuts through the extremely tough basaltic rock of an ancient lava flow. This crescent-shaped gorge is about 80 miles long and reaches depths of 4,000 feet. It contained a series of rapids that early French traders and explorers called "Les Dalles," or the trough. Native Americans and later fur traders found this natural break in navigation a convenient place to trade. The famed explorers Lewis and Clark described the Dalles as the "Great Mart" of the whole region.

In addition to its economic functions, however, the great trough was extremely important to both Native Americans and all posterity. It was a museum of the history and culture of all the people who passed through the land over time. The section of the Dalles that was submerged as waters rose behind the dam was also known as Petroglyph Canyon.

Many of the petroglyphs are readily recognized as elk, bighorn sheep, owls, and eagles. These images may have been created as part of magical ceremonies to bring more game to hunters. Other pictures, however, are more mysterious, involving geometric forms or unrecognizable symbols.

When it became known that the construction of the Dalles Dam would submerge all the rock art of the gorge, local Native Americans expressed outrage over this destruction of their artistic and spiritual heritage. It would be an act of senseless vandalism. The comparison was made to a great library that held the only copies of all humanity's history, dreams, and beliefs. Would we tolerate an arsonist wandering about this library, randomly burning volumes of irreplaceable knowledge and wisdom?

Archeologists say that the canyon has been occupied for at least ten thousand years. Surviving petroglyphs date from as recently as two hundred years to as far in the past as three thousand years. Many of the symbols, both lost and saved, are difficult to decipher. Few petroglyphs could be salvaged from the rising waters, as they had to be sawn from the solid rock and moved to other locations. Archeologists, historians, and Native American shamans, along with mystics and spiritualists of all races, still argue varying interpretations of the few surviving remnants of the once vast library of tribal folklore recorded on the rocks. Columbia Hills State Park's Temani Pesh-wa Trail, for example, displays the namesake petroglyph, Temani Pesh-wa, or "She Who Watches." Who does she represent?

What are we to make of the threatening "River Devil"? Was he, as believed by some, warning of invaders (white settlers) traveling down the great river from the east?

Some contemporary spiritual visionaries agree with tribal shamans, past and present, that these weird forms and symbols were intended to give insight into the future as well as the past. Some petroglyphs, it has been asserted, warned of Mount St. Helen's catastrophic 1980 eruption, which blew smoke and ash 80,000 feet into the air and released a mile-wide avalanche that killed fifty-seven people in a sparsely populated region that had already been evacuated.

Is it true, as some tribal historians believe, that among the lost symbols of drowned petroglyphs were predictions of a future explosion of Mount Rainier, which could endanger hundreds of thousands of people? Many believe that the canyon's lost symbols could provide additional support to the Mayan calendar's doomsday predictions for the near future. What if they're right and the clues lie underwater and are thus unreadable?

The Most Horrific Ghosts

You really, really do not want to see these apparitions. Not even for a second. The sight of this pair of ghosts is thought to have caused gut-wrenching nightmares among observers, nightmares that persisted for years afterward, despite psychiatric treatment. The phantoms of the infamous Whitman Massacre surely must be the most awesomely frightening apparitions in Washington State, if not the nation.

The vaporous, gruesome duo are the shades of Marcus and Narcissa Whitman, founders of an ill-fated mission to the Cayuse and Umatilla Indians of eastern Washington. The Whitmans had led the first major wagon train along the famed Oregon Trail. Despite the clearly hostile attitude of local Indians, and contrary to the advice of experienced guides, the Whitmans determined to establish a mission at a place called Waiilatpu, about seven miles west of the present town of Walla Walla. The crudely constructed mission was built in 1836. For eleven years, the Whitmans tirelessly sought to convert their Native American neighbors. Then, on November 29, 1847, disaster struck. The Whitmans and thirteen other whites were ruthlessly slaughtered. Fifty-four other women and children were kidnapped and held for ransom, which eventually was paid by the nearby Hudsons Bay Trading Post, despite the deaths in captivity of several prisoners.

The spirits of Marcus and Narcissa take the forms of their horribly disfigured corpses on the morning they died. Dr. Whitman, a trained physician, had been called out of his house by Indians who said they needed medical treatment and advice. As soon as he appeared, he was set upon and hacked to death with axes, his body dismembered and mutilated. When his wife rushed out, responding to screams, she was shot in the face.

What caused such a violent display of outraged hatred and disdain? The Whitman massacre might be an extreme example of culture clash between the Native Americans and the rapidly multiplying, invading white settlers.

Dr. Whitman had promised to do his best to cure the diseases then rampant among the Indians, who had no natural immunity against diseases brought by Europeans. Measles spread quickly, and fatally, among the Indians, followed by outbreaks of cholera. Dr. Whitman's medicine could not save the victims of these diseases. It had been a tradition among local tribes to reward or punish their shamans in accordance with results of promised cures. The death of a patient who had been promised a cure could be a death sentence for the shaman.

This situation was complicated by the activities of a rogue white trader named Joe Lewis. Lewis was a malicious character who plotted to turn the Indians against the Whitmans. He evidently hoped that the disillusioned Indians would drive the Whitmans out of their

mission, allowing Lewis to ransack it. Lewis told the Indians that Dr. Whitman was poisoning them with his medicines. The already suspicious Indians reacted in an orgy of violence, setting off a war with settlers in the vicinity that lasted until 1858.

The group of graves and a large crypt sealed with a massive stone lie near the reconstructed mission. It is here that the specters of the Whitmans appear, early in the mornings. The butchered remains of Marcus Whitman are barely recognizable as once human. The disjointed parts seem to be slightly misty in appearance. The severed limbs, torso, and head are all covered in blood. Narcissa's face is ruined beyond description by point-blank bullet wounds. These ephemeral images testify to the savagery of their deaths. The gruesome phantoms fade, leaving only the lonely winds.

Sounds of Violent Death

It is after midnight, on a weekday evening. The building is quiet; indeed, the whole campus is quiet, as the school year is over. Summer sessions are a week away here at Washington State University in Pullman. The green rolling hills of the 600-acre campus are almost too quiet—as though the whole neighborhood was holding its breath, waiting for the screams, hoping the screams wouldn't come again this night.

Then, from the dusty bowels of Stevens Hall comes the dreaded screaming. The first blast of sound is clearly that of a young woman's terrified reaction to her captor's advance. That first voicing of unimaginable horror is clear and forceful. Then the scream becomes literally strangled, as was the woman herself. The tragic sounds diminish to agonized, gasping moans, then barely perceptible whimpers, then silence. The silence is the worst part, say those unfortunate enough to have heard the whole ghostly sequence. The silence signifies the final end of an innocent young life. It is as though a candle—no, a firecracker—had been snuffed out before it reached its glorious potential.

The screaming ghost lives on in legend at the university. Her identity is unknown, her fate uncertain, and her final resting place undiscovered. Was she ever a real, living person? Those who've heard the tortured sounds of her spirit reliving her last moments have no doubts. They can never forget those screams that now seem etched on their souls.

According to local legend, a young woman, a student at the university, was staying, quite illegally, in the basement of Stevens Hall. The building was closed after graduation, not to reopen until the beginning of the fall semester. But there she was, apparently expert at keeping out of sight; only a few close friends knew she was there. It was her isolation that proved fatal.

Her secretive existence meant that no one immediately missed her. The grim surmise is that somehow Gary Ridgway, the infamous Green River Killer, had learned that she was hiding alone in the basement of Stevens Hall. An isolated, lovely young woman, vulnerable and easily overwhelmed, appealed to Ridgway's macabre, twisted taste. Could the mysterious hideaway have been yet another victim of the Green River Killer? Some circumstances point to this serial killer; others appear to be contradictory.

Ridgway confessed and was convicted of the murders of forty-eight young women between 1982 and his arrest on November 30, 2002. The bodies of most of his victims were disposed of in the Green River or along its banks. Most of these murders took place in the SeaTac area, where Ridgway had grown up. His known victims were prostitutes or teenage runaways, socially isolated and readily victimized. Is it likely that the Green River Killer would also be guilty of a murder at the opposite end of the state? Supposedly, serial killers all the way back to Jack the Ripper have a "comfort zone," a geographical area with which they are familiar and in which they operate.

But Ridgway enjoyed taunting the police and everyone else. He repeatedly changed his patterns. Part of his plea agreement to avoid execution was that he would lead police to the locations of his buried victims. He lied. Some bodies were left in plain sight, others were craftily hidden. Most were nude, some not. He admitted transporting two victims to Portland, Oregon, just to confuse police. He deliberately broke his own patterns of behavior to toy with his pursuers. He confessed to forty-eight murders but police believe he killed at least nine more. He himself later claimed seventy-one in all, but refused to give any details. Ridgway has said that murder was his career. Clearly it is possible that the screaming ghost in Stevens Hall could be that of one of his many unknown victims.

Is the periodic manifestation of the Stevens Hall ghost a reminder that evil, pure evil, is all too real? Some who've heard this soundtrack of violent death believe so.

The Walla Walla Banshee

The bitter winter winds seem to moan as they sweep across the lonely countryside just south and west of Walla Walla. There are few natural obstacles to the passage of the winds, and the sound seems to change with the speed. Is it just imagination that the winds sometimes seem to cry out, even to scream? That might depend on whether you believe in banshees, for those who do believe have heard the unearthly cry of the Walla Walla Banshee.

Banshees are prominent supernatural beings in Irish and Scottish folk traditions. They are female in voice and form, and tradition says that they either appear or cry out in warning that sudden, violent death is about to come calling. In ancient Celtic tradition, a banshee was a kind of family oracle. Each family had its own banshee, which would appear or cry in advance of a death in that family. In some legends, the banshee takes the form of a beautiful young woman with long hair worn loose, streaming in the wind. She wears a red, green, or white dress. Her eyes are bright red from crying in mourning. If seen, she will not be heard; if her distinctive wails are heard in the wind, she will not materialize. In some tales, the banshee takes the form of an old, ugly hag who is seen washing blood off of clothing in a nearby stream.

The Walla Walla Banshee has been Americanized; it is not associated with any one family but with one particularly horrific event. Walla Walla was a pretty wild place in the 1860s, a supply point and resort of sorts for prospectors heading for the gold fields of Idaho. "Rough and ready" was the town's motto: saloons, gambling joints, and brothels thrived in uncontrolled, lawless exuberance. Murder and mayhem were everyday occurrences.

Soon, self-appointed vigilantes began to fight back, but some of them cared little about things like civil rights, impartial juries, witnesses, or solid proof. Theirs was simply a counterreign of violence. Doubtless, most of the men they hanged deserved their death sentence, but not all.

A prospector named Tim O'Grady was celebrating finding gold. He was doing his hard-drinking, hard-playing routine in the Last Chance Saloon. An argument broke out and a man was shot. It was not clear if Tim acted in self-defense or not. The vigilantes decided to hang Tim, mostly because he was a drunken stranger. "You've no right to hang me!" protested Tim. "I'm an innocent man and an Irishman too."

The vigilantes decided, drunk themselves, that indeed they wouldn't hang an Irishman—they'd drown him. Tim's hands and feet were bound, and he was thrown into the river. He drowned, screaming a chain of Irish curses on the overzealous vigilantes. As evening fell, a young woman, dressed all in red, appeared to rise out of the mists that covered the water's surface. Her bright red eyes glared at the vigilantes who were watching. Her long hair fanned out on the surface of the water as she silently pointed to each and every spectator. She disappeared from view as the eerie moaning and wailing began. Complaining of nonstop banshee wailing in his ears, the ringleader of the vigilantes shot himself dead the next day. It is said that several other vigilantes, driven insane by incessant wailing that others could not hear, were institutionalized for the rest of their lives.

To this day, the Walla Walla Banshee is supposed to cry and moan in the ears of anyone who has condemned another without a fair hearing.

The Neverending Quest

The glitter of gold and the dream of sudden riches has driven men to cross continents and oceans. It has also driven men insane with frustrated greed. It is said that the spirit of one victim of "gold fever," the powerful compulsion to find the precious metal at all costs, is still searching for his gold—gold that was found, then lost again.

Washington's gold rush is not as famous as those of California or Alaska, but it did happen. Eastern Washington territory, which at the time included what is now northern Idaho, had its gold rush from the late 1850s through the 1870s. In 1862 alone, seven million dollars worth of gold passed through the assay office in Walla Walla. Placer gold, or flecks and nuggets of pure gold, was found in the sands and gravels of the Snake River and many of the little streams emptying into it.

Unlike hard rock, or lode mining, placer mining requires little experience and very simple equipment; a shovel and a pie plate will do. A pan is filled with river gravel and agitated in running water, which washes away the lighter material and allows heavy gold particles to remain behind.

The story is that three friends were canoeing on the Snake River, about 70 miles south of Clarkston, when their canoe beached on a sandbar at the mouth of a small tributary creek. The men got out of the canoe to push it back into deeper water when they saw bright yellow nuggets gleaming in the shallows. They quickly filled a pail with gold. They were jubilant but now faced a problem. They needed supplies of shovels, tents, and food to work the claim they must register. They decided to bury most of the gold on the shore and go to Walla Walla to outfit themselves for some serious gold panning. Showing up with a lot of gold, they reasoned, would invite interest from the wrong type of people.

Their precautions failed to protect them. The three prospectors, on reaching Walla Walla, decided on a celebratory drink before doing their shopping. One drink became three or four; alcohol-loosened tongues revealed the discovery. One of the trio was shot dead. The two survivors retreated to a boardinghouse, where a week later one died of "natural causes," a catchall category in those days before forensic science applied to anyone whose corpse was not perforated with bullet holes. The lone survivor believed that his friend had been poisoned; he wisely decided to leave town and lie low for a while. This man, "Cockeyed Jack" Moran, disappeared from the historic record, but evidently not from the supernatural history of the Snake River country.

Out of the deepening shadows of twilight, the figure appears along the river banks of the Snake between Clarkston and Asotin. A man in his late twenties, he is wearing the costume of a mid-nineteenth-century prospector: a plaid woolen shirt, heavy canvas trousers, and stout boots. He wears an unkempt black beard. His left eye stares fixedly off to the left, while his right eye scans the riverbank. Repeatedly, he stops to dig a shallow hole with his well-worn shovel. Finding nothing, he snorts in disgust, walks on a few more paces, and then stops to dig yet another hole. Oddly, the holes seem to refill with dirt on their own. Surely, this is the ghost of Cockeyed Jack, still looking for his long-lost stash of gold nuggets.

As soon as this specter senses a living being nearby, he glares at the intruder on his neverending quest, and brandishes his shovel in a threatening manner. At this point, it would be best to retreat. Jack is badly frustrated about still not being able to retrieve his buried gold. Legend has it that no one else had better find his gold either or they'll be haunted by Cockeyed Jack for the rest of their lives.

Bibliography

Books

American Automobile Association. *Oregon and Washington Tour Book.* Heathrow, FL: AAA Publishing, 2009.

Beckley, Timothy. *The UFO Silencers.* New Brunswick, NJ: Inner Light, 1990.

Botkin, B. A., ed. *A Treasury of American Folklore.* New York: Crown Publishers, 1944.

Clark, Jerome. *Unexplained!* Canton, MI: Visible Ink Press, 1999.

Coleman, Loren. *Mysterious America.* London: Faber and Faber, 1983.

Daegling, David. *Bigfoot Exposed.* Walnut Creek, CA: Altamira Press, 2004.

Davis, Jefferson. *Ghosts and Strange Critters of Washington and Oregon.* Vancouver, WA: Norseman Ventures, 1999.

Dorson, Richard. *American Folklore.* Chicago: University of Chicago Press, 1959.

Epting, Chris. *The Birthplace Book: A Guide to Birth Sites of Famous People, Places and Things.* Mechanicsburg, PA: Stackpole Books, 2009.

Green, John. *Encounters with Bigfoot.* Surrey, BC: Hancock House, 1994.

Guiley, Rosemary Ellen. *The Encyclopedia of Ghosts and Spirits.* New York: Facts on File, 1992.

Harper, Charles. *Haunted Houses: Tales of the Supernatural.* Philadelphia: J. B. Lippincott, 1930.

Hauck, Dennis. *Haunted Places: The National Directory.* New York: Penguin Putnam, 2002.

Krantz, Grover. *Bigfoot/Sasquatch Evidence.* Surrey, BC: Hancock House, 1999.

Krantz, Les. *America by the Numbers: Facts and Figures from the Weighty to the Way-Out.* Boston: Houghton Mifflin, 1993.

Myers, Arthur. *A Ghosthunter's Guide to Haunted Landmarks, Parks, Churches, and Other Public Places.* Chicago: Contemporary Books, 1993.

————. *The Ghostly Register*. New York: McGraw-Hill/Contemporary Books, 1986.

MacDonald, Margaret. *Ghost Stories from the Pacific Northwest*. Little Rock, AR: August House, 1995.

Mack, John. *Abduction: Human Encounters with Aliens*. New York: Scribners, 1994.

Norman, Michael, and Beth Scott. *Historic Haunted America*. New York: Tor, 1995.

Pickering, David. *Casell Dictionary of Superstitions*. London: Casell, 1995.

Roosevelt, Theodore. *Wilderness Hunter*. Vol. 2. New York: G. P. Putnam, 1893.

Skinner, Charles. *American Myths and Legends*. Detroit: Gale Research Co., 1974.

Stein, George, ed. *The Encyclopedia of the Paranormal*. Buffalo: Prometheus, 1996.

Strong, Emory. *Stone Age on the Columbia River*. Portland, OR: Binford and Mort, 1959.

Taylor, Troy. *The Haunting of America: Ghosts and Legends from America's Past*. Alton, IL: Whitechapel Productions, 2001.

Thompson, C. J. S. *The Mystery and Lore of Apparitions*. London: Harold Shaylor, 1930.

Writers Program of the Works Projects Administration. *Washington: A Guide to the Evergreen State*. American Guide Series. Rev. ed. Portland, OR: Binford and Mort, 1950.

Websites

GhostsandCritters.com/WashingtonGhosts.html
GhostEyes.com
AmericanFolklore.net/ff.html
LegendsofAmerica.com/GH-celebrityghosts2.html
TheShadowLands.net/Places/Washington.html

Acknowledgments

THIS IS MY ELEVENTH BOOK WRITTEN UNDER THE SKILLFUL EDITORIAL guidance and friendly encouragement of Kyle Weaver; he has become a true friend and wise counselor. Brett Keener guided the manuscript through the production process with his usual careful attention and professional expertise. The illustrations are the product of Marc Radle's impressive imagination and artistic talents.

Elizabeth Eckardt once again demonstrated her amazing ability to turn my handwritten scrawls into a polished manuscript; many thanks, Liz. Steve Eckardt kept my laptop healthy and obedient. His knowledge is matched by his patience with a computer novice; many thanks, Steve.

My good friend and colleague Chet Zimolzak accompanied me on a field trip that took us from the Columbia Gorge and Mount St. Helens to Olympia, Tacoma, Seattle, and the Olympic Mountains. Good friends Janet and Lowell Peterson of Graham, Washington, gave me many good ideas and generously shared their files on the wonders and mysteries of their native state.

I wish to thank the experts at the Washington State Tourism Office of the Department of Community, Trade, and Economic Development and the State Parks and Recreation Commission, both in Olympia, and all the various county and city tourism offices and chambers of commerce.

I appreciate the friendly and efficient assistance of the professional librarians at the McGowan Library in Pitman, the Gloucester County Library in Mullica Hill, and the Campbell Library at Rowan University in Glassboro. My good friend Herb Richardson helped locate source materials.

Once again, my dear Diane lovingly tolerated the semipermanent, confused clutter of books and papers that accompanies a writing project. Thanks for your love and patience my darling.

About the Author

CHARLES A. STANSFIELD JR. TAUGHT GEOGRAPHY AT ROWAN UNIVERSITY in Glassboro, New Jersey, for forty-one years and published fifteen textbooks on cultural and regional geography. In the course of his research, he realized that stories of ghosts and other strange phenomena reflect the history, culture, economy, and even physical geography of a region. He is the author of *Haunted Presidents* and eight titles in the Stackpole Books Haunted Series: *Haunted Arizona, Haunted Northern California, Haunted Southern California, Haunted Ohio, Haunted Vermont, Haunted Maine, Haunted Jersey Shore,* and *Haunted New Jersey.*